# THE THEORY OF AMERICAN LITERATURE

# THE THEORY OF

# *American*

# *Literature*

HOWARD MUMFORD JONES

HARVARD UNIVERSITY

*Cornell University Press*

ITHACA, NEW YORK, 1948

PRINTED IN THE UNITED STATES OF AMERICA BY THE
VAIL-BALLOU PRESS, INC., BINGHAMTON, NEW YORK

For WILLIAM CHARVAT

# Preface

DOUBTLESS there exists somewhere a thorough survey of the problem of American literary history, but the only work I have seen is in Hungarian (a language I cannot read) by Országh László, *Az Amerikai Irodalomtörténetíras Fejlödése* (Budapest, 1935), which means "The Development of the Histories of American Literature." When this was translated to me by a Hungarian student, it seemed to me more suggestive than scholarly, and is, among other things, a product of the nineteen-twenties. There is a thoughtful article by Robert E. Spiller, "The Task of the Historian of American Literature," in the *Sewanee Review* for 1935, and various essays on various aspects of the problem have been published by other critics and scholars. But the ways by which we have, in Mr. Spiller's phrase, sought to establish "that new race of American literary historians, who must be philosophers and economists as well as critics" have not, so far as I am aware, been examined in their historical framework until now.

The origin of these pages was as lectures on the Messenger Foundation at Cornell University in December, 1947. I owe much to the stimulation of my kindly and attentive audiences.

# PREFACE

I am indebted to William Charvat, Kenneth B. Murdock, Douglas Bush, and Henry A. Myers for thoughtful comment on my manuscript; and I am grateful to Priscilla Shames and Louise R. Olsen for their patient labors as research assistants. I am also indebted to Ross Borden and Richard Ludwig for their work with proof and index, and to Mrs. Chester Noyes Greenough for kindly giving me access to the notes on colonial literature left by Professor Greenough. Phoebe Donald brought expert knowledge to the editing of the manuscript. But above all I am indebted to "my Bessie" for aid, opposition, and advice.

For permission to reprint somewhat lengthy extracts of works still in copyright I am indebted to Appleton-Century-Crofts, Inc., in the case of William P. Trent's *History of American Literature*, and to Henry Holt and Co., Inc., for Henry S. Pancoast's *Introduction to American Literature*.

In order to simplify the index I have listed only those names which have a direct bearing upon the problem of literary history.

HOWARD MUMFORD JONES

*Harvard University*
*June 5, 1948*

# Contents

# THE THEORY OF AMERICAN LITERATURE

# I

# "The Literary Spirit of Each Age"

IN OFFERING these essays on literary history I am conscious of the unpopularity into which this form of scholarship has fallen. The present cry is for criticism; and a rising generation of English scholars is nothing if not critical, in both senses of the word. Yielding to the fascination of Croce, of T. S. Eliot, of I. A. Richards, of C. S. Lewis, they have not felt the fascination of Taine, of Brunetière, of Meinecke, of Brandes, of Menéndez y Pelayo, of W. P. Ker, of Moses Coit Tyler. They have revolted against the naïveté of parallel passages, but they have fallen under the spell of textual analysis—so much so that one contemporary teacher admiringly remarks of an essay by another that never before has the text of a poem been subjected to such exhaustive scrutiny. Whether the pleasures of literature are more diminished by parallelism or by probing is a nice question I shall not attempt to determine.

Yet what has happened to the higher study of literature amusingly illustrates the platitude that you cannot escape history. Ours is the age of psychology; and critics, children of this age, have been profoundly impressed by the intricate relations discoverable between form and psychology, between meaning and expression, between a writer's awareness of the certainties and confusions of his life and

1

his attempt to phrase or symbolize these sureties and con-
flicts. Accordingly, they have devoted enormous energy
to hunting out recondite meanings in poems that have
sometimes had these meanings, and to discovering myth
in prose that comes to carry metaphysical burdens its
author may not have intended. In short, a vast new glossing
of texts appears in the name of criticism, an example of
which is the accumulation of encyclopedic lore about
Joyce's *Ulysses.* As a literary historian I am reminded that in
Alexandria scholars also went in for glosses, producing that
hieratic library which paved the road to Byzantium. And
as a reader I think that books are made for men, not men
for books; that we read for direct pleasure, for simple statement; and that except in university reviews the human
animal takes the printed page calmly and not as a problem
in casuistry.

The critics to whom I refer have been honorably moved
by the tragic problems of the twentieth century and have
honorably concerned themselves, not merely with aesthetic
considerations, but also with moral evil and with good.
This, too, is a historic act, one which links them with Den-
nis and Rymer. But the moral teaching satisfactory to this
criticism is curiously limited. Its sacred writings are a
small portion of seventeenth-century literature and a small
library supposed to be written in apostolic succession
thereto. We learn over and over again of the virtues of
Donne, of Milton, of Dostoevski, of Melville, of Kierke-
gaard, of Henry James, and of Joyce, but we learn nothing
of the sunny humanity of Burns, of Dickens, of Miss Austen,
of Thackeray, of Turgenev, of Hugo, of Björnson, of H. G.
Wells. The first group possesses, we are told, an "imaginative vision of evil." But literature also includes an imagi-

2

native vision of good, not to speak of a vision of the truth that human life is neither wholly good nor wholly evil but a mixture more like a rag rug than the famous pattern in the Jamesian carpet. Parenthetically, the literary historian may express some bewilderment before criticism directed to moral evil and to good which seems never to recur directly to that supreme moral masterpiece in English literature, the King James Bible. Why is Joyce more illuminating than Job?

But though the exploitation of a small shelf of books and the elimination of the rest of the world's vast library may amuse the literary historian, it does not amaze him. He is used to it. Contemporary criticism repeats a familiar pattern. The friends of Boileau could find little virtue in anything written between the Silver Age of Latin letters and the Augustan Age of Louis XIV; the period of Schlegel, on the other hand, obliterated the entire *Aufklärung* and returned with loving delight to its own version of the Middle Ages. Objective criticism is as whimsical today as objective criticism usually is; and the fact that much of it is written by university men does not mean that it is universal.

This criticism has undoubtedly extended the range of sensibility among a few. It has taught us to read some sorts of texts more carefully. It has underlined the patent truth that the philological and social approaches to belles-lettres are limited. It has seen that historical explanation is not explication. But it is also precious and remote. One may mischievously conjecture what Dr. Johnson, who found the biographical parts of literature attracted him most, would say concerning the assumption that the facts of an author's career are irrelevant to the pure understanding of poetry. One can only patiently recall that

Sainte-Beuve devotes his *Causeries* as often to figures who did not count as major writers as he did to literary geniuses. Is it not true that if you go all the way with some of Croce's disciples and remove historical perspective from literary art, you usually have very little art left? Even if you concentrate upon types of ambiguity or the creation of myth or problems of tension and release, you are presently forced back upon an understanding of taste, of style, of culture, of society itself. The persistent effort of academic criticism to find a usable past—that is, a past which shall be mainly an extension of the twentieth century—is an engaging tribute to history.

The revolt against literary history goes back at least a quarter of a century. I do not know who began this Thirty Years War, but I select at random a sentence by T. S. Eliot, written in 1920, as illuminating the conflict. Mr. Eliot then wrote that "the whole of the literature of Europe from Homer . . . has a simultaneous existence and composes a simultaneous order." [1] In one sense, as Byron remarks of another platitude, this is extremely true. You can go into any large library and ask for Homer and for Damon Runyon, get them both, and read them simultaneously for the light they cast on each other. And they will mutually cast light. But it is in another sense fallacious. Mr. Eliot inferentially denies the primacy of literary history to the study of literature. But though it may be true in a metaphysical sense that in the subject-object relationship of transcendental philosophy the past exists only as we think of it in the knife-edge present and only as the Pure Reason imposes order upon it, this philosophical commonplace does not help criticism and does not help history, and its results have been disastrous for both. They have been disastrous because adherence to the principle encourages whimsical and private views of the past. The seventeenth century which criticism of this order creates is so remote from the actual seventeenth century as to become but a projection of the contemporary world viewed by contemporary criticism. For that great age, if it produced John Donne and John Milton, produced also Francis Bacon and John Locke, Tom Brown of facetious memory, Durfey's *Pills to Purge Melancholy*, the highfalutin romances beloved of Dorothy Osborne, and the writings of Dryden and Defoe.

Criticism extends its whimsicality to American literature. A few writers—Hawthorne, Thoreau, Melville, Henry Adams are examples—are permitted to be present in simultaneous existence and simultaneous order, as if they only or principally were the strength and value of the American literary tradition. It is still a historical truth that the vision of good in Longfellow once satisfied the world, that the novels of Cooper influenced writers as disparate as Balzac and Karl Postl; that the popularity of Mark Twain rests upon *Innocents Abroad* and *Roughing It* quite as much as upon *The Mysterious Stranger;* and that the chief American poet to wrestle with the good and evil of evolution was not Hart Crane but William Vaughn Moody. Academic criticism has a faintly apologetic air whenever it is compelled to refer to such thoroughly American performances as *John Brown's Body*, Bryant's "Prairies," or *Uncle Tom's Cabin*, which, if ever a book created a myth, is a supreme example of mythology. But when criticism grows subjective, history becomes one-sided.

The nineteenth century is par excellence the century academic criticism wishes to destroy. Only Keats and Coleridge at one end of that epoch, only Arnold in the

5

middle, only Hopkins at its termination seem worth discussing. Macaulay, Tennyson, Browning, Dickens, George Eliot, Meredith, the pre-Raphaelites, Carlyle, Ruskin, Spencer, Mill were mistaken men and women. The age of Victoria was wrong-headed, superficial, shallow, trivial, hypocritical, genteel, bourgeois, and much else. Its theory of poetry was romantic and wrong; its prose may have been what Oliver Elton calls it, "noble," but it was a vulgar nobility; its belief in progress was a colossal error which only a few persons like Thomas Hardy and James Thomson managed to penetrate. But penetration did not improve their styles. Above all, that century was the age of spiritual decay, a century which, ignorant of the sublime abysses into which humanity can sink, mistakenly exalted man to impossible moral heights.

If there were time, it would be interesting to inquire whether the vision of moral evil and of good in *Faust*, most characteristic of nineteenth-century poems, is not on the whole saner than that in the novels of Kafka and Joyce, but to do so were to lead us astray; and it is sufficient to remark that inasmuch as one of the great contributions of the nineteenth century to thought was the genetic approach to values, literary history, which is essentially genetic, now suffers from the general anti-Victorianism of academic criticism. And the reason I begin with a digression concerning criticism is that we shall not understand the complicated problem of American literary history unless we abandon current attempts to ignore the nineteenth century. Let us commence by granting to that rich and vital age the right to live in its own time, and accept from it the wisdom it has to give.

6

2

There is, however, no necessary hostility between literary history and literary criticism, the substance of one being the food of the other, although I confess academic reformers sometimes seem desirous of creating enmity. But we cannot, I repeat, get on with our story unless, ignoring the prejudices I have described, we accept the nineteenth century as something more than a regrettable hiatus between John Donne and John Crowe Ransom. For in English, at any rate, and, indeed, in Europe generally, literary history was the creation of the nineteenth century. Its theoretical foundations were laid by Bacon, but practice did not pass beyond primitive performance until almost the end of the eighteenth century. The first edition of Tiraboschi's *Storia della letteratura italiana,* perhaps the earliest literary history we can still consult with pleasure, was not completed until 1781. In that year was also published the final volume of the first literary history in English worthy of the name, Warton's *History of English Poetry.* Nothing approximating a history of American letters was printed until 1824–1825, when John Neal, then in England, contributed to *Blackwood's Magazine* a series of hazy papers on such American authors as he could remember. Perhaps we ought rather to refer our beginning to the publication of Samuel L. Knapp's *Lectures on American Literature* at New York in 1829. Almost our entire library of literary history (as distinct from collections of biographies, anthologies, books of commentary, and the like *biblia a biblia*), so far as modern literatures are concerned, comes after that immense alteration of values which, focusing in the French

Revolution, flows from it with gathering force as the nineteenth century wears on.

In an unfavorable sense one may say that nationalism and history wed together, patriotism and pedagogy kissed each other when many of these books were born. But to say only this would be to reduce scholarship to dialectical materialism. We can no more dismiss literary history as irrelevant than we can dismiss history as irrelevant. Men such as Hettner, Lanson, Sir Leslie Stephen, Ticknor, and De Sanctis cannot be put by as if they were each like Johnson's lexicographer, a harmless necessary drudge. They and their fellows have created tools for our use that an epoch so recent as the age of Napoleon was still struggling to invent.

But let me exhibit the Emersonian virtue of inconsistency. If academic criticism needs the correction of literary history, younger scholars nevertheless can allege a very strong point on their side and win at least a debater's victory. The great weakness of literary history is that nobody quite knows what it is. Of course there is also violent disagreement about the postulates of literary criticism, but literary history is in a worse state of confusion since it includes not one Great Unknown, but two. "History" and "literature" are terms the meaning of which everybody knows, but the definition of which nobody can give.

Take, for example, the concept "history." Is history such a codification and examination of documents emanating from the past as will establish or illustrate general laws? Or is it a method of objective fact finding? What, then, is the relation between the objective fact and the governing laws? Is the historian to "divest himself of all philosophical, religious, political, economic, social, sexual, moral, and aesthetic interests so that he can view facts with strict impartiality?" Or is he an imaginative artist, intuiting the motives of men long dead and revealing them in dramatic narrative by literary means? A writer in 1940, discussing this ancient controversy, concludes that history as a science is even yet not established.[2]

Let us not spend time on that even vaguer term, "literature," but simply note that "literary history" is a cloudier concept still. One can perhaps define it as an orderly record of those written works (and of pertinent facts about them) mankind values or has valued in the past, but such a statement tells us nothing. Yet, as soon as one steps beyond it, one is in Cloud-cuckoo-land. There the haze is so general that Professor René Wellek, distinguished investigator in this field, remarks at the opening of a penetrating essay on literary history that "routine, confusion, resignation, and scepticism seem to characterize the present attitude" toward the subject. He suggests five points for clarification. We need a clearer realization of methods and aims. We need to synthesize and co-ordinate work already accomplished. We ought, he thinks, to restrict attempts to account for literature in terms of something else, and expect less from an excessive determinism which would reduce literature to a mirror of some other human activity. We ought to concentrate on the study of the actual work of art. And we ought, finally, to write literary history as a work of art itself.[3]

No one can reasonably quarrel with his excellent admonitions. Some of these suggestions—for example, the advice to synthesize present research and to write history as a work of art—apply generally to historical writing and have value in that larger field as well. Others—for example,

9

the admonitions to study the work as art and to account for it in terms of itself and not in terms of social determinism—touch the central problem of any history of any art; namely, how shall the more or less private evaluations we call criticism be fused with that more or less public affair, the reputation and temporal significance of any work of art important enough to be chronicled? With no desire to evade the implications of Professor Wellek's program, I remind you that literary history is almost the youngest of historical forms, and that it is neither astonishing nor disheartening to find disagreement about method, imprecision in the use of terms, or dogmatic assertion of contradictions. Were history a consistent and logical act, we should not have innumerable essays on the art of historiography, to which almost every meeting of the American Historical Association adds another. We do not abolish departments of psychology because a dozen battles over primary assumptions rage in this field, nor argue that philosophy is useless because in metaphysics two of a trade so seldom agree.

3

Possibly an inherent ambiguity has haunted literary history from its foundation. For when we go back to Bacon, we find in the *De Augmentis Scientiarum* many of the problems that Professor Wellek finds it necessary still to discuss. Bacon demands a "complete and universal history of Learning." Such a history, he says, would "very greatly assist the wisdom and skill of learned men in the use and administration of learning," for it would "exhibit the movements and perturbations, the virtues and vices which take place no less in intellectual than in civil matters." It was his hope that "from the observation of these the best system of government might be derived and established."

When it came to particularizing the mode of such a history, Bacon was full and explicit:

The argument is no other than to inquire and collect out of the records of all times what particular kinds of learning and art have flourished in what ages and regions of the world; their antiquities, their progresses, their migrations (for sciences migrate like nations) over the different parts of the globe; and again their decays, disappearances and revivals. The occasion and origin of each art should likewise be observed; the manner and system of transmission, and the plan and order of study and practice. To these should be added a history of the sects, and the principal controversies in which learned men have been engaged, the calumnies to which they have been exposed, the praises and honours by which they have been rewarded; an account of the principal authors, books, schools, successions, academies, societies, colleges, orders,—in a word, everything which relates to the state of learning. Above all things (for this is the ornament and life of Civil History) I wish events to be coupled with their causes. I mean, that an account should be given of the characters of the several regions and peoples; their natural disposition, whether apt and suited for the study of learning, or unfitted and indifferent to it; the accidents of the times, whether adverse or propitious to science; the emulations and infusions of different religions; the enmity or partiality of laws; the eminent virtues and services of individual persons in the promotion of learning, and the like. Now all this I would have handled in a historical way, not wasting time, after the manner of critics, in praise and blame, but simply narrating the past historically, with but slight intermixture of private judgment.

For the *manner* of compiling such a history I particularly advise that the matter and provision of it be not drawn from histories and commentaries alone; but that the principal books written in each century, or perhaps shorter periods, proceeding in regular order from the earliest ages, be themselves taken into consultation; that so (I do not say a complete perusal, for that would be an endless labour, but) by testing them here and there, the Literary Spirit of each age may be charmed, as it were, from the dead.

I have quoted the standard translation of Bacon's Latin.[4] It may not be amiss to remark that "colleges" in this passage does not mean a college of liberal arts but a professional body as in "college of physicians"; "sciences" refers to any body of organized knowledge, not to the physical and natural sciences only; and, since it was inconceivable to Renaissance thought that an unlettered man could produce a book, that "learning" in this passage includes both scholarship and the practice of belles-lettres. Bacon's slurring reference to "critics" "wasting time" is, moreover, no condemnation of literary criticism but only of that fault-finding habit we associate with pedantry.

But once we have adjusted ourselves to these small peculiarities, we must be struck by the fact that in short compass Bacon summarized most of the problems which still trouble literary history. Sound literary history can proceed only from original records of art and learning and from an examination of the principal books written in each century, but Bacon notes the impossibility of a "complete perusal" even of these and proposes a practical method of charming the literary spirit of a given age. All literature is the joint production of author and reader, since, as Professor Guérard puts it, he who voyages through strange seas of thought alone is not acclaimed a poet until his return;[5] Bacon therefore proposes that literary history shall include both individual persons of "eminent virtues and services" to literature, and also the race, the environment, and the historical moment—to use Taine's famous distinctions. We must, says Bacon, consider "the characters of the several regions and peoples" and their natural disposition, whether "suited for learning or not"—in other words, the linguistic, cultural, or national tradition in which a book is born; we must consider the "occasion" of literature, the "state of learning" in place and time, the religious and political structures of a society, and those institutions which create or enrich literature and learning.

Moreover, the genetic problem, central to literary history, is also in Bacon. Are there cycles of growth and decay in literary art? Are genres subject to evolution as Brunetière and John Addington Symonds believed? Or is it true in Wellek's phrase that "art has always reached its goal"? Bacon had foreseen these questions in his demand for a history that shall chronicle the antiquities, progresses, migrations, decays, disappearances, and revivals of learning, the "manner and system of transmission, and the plan and order of study and practice" of literature, not to speak of the relation between literature and other forms of culture. And, finally, he had foreseen the problem of fusing historical objectivity and private taste.

But I think the supreme and central fact in Bacon's essay is that literature is a social act. This does not mean that every piece of literature must have social significance. But no poet is an island unto himself. The purest of pure poetry may be intended for the purest of rarefied readers, but it is still meant for an audience living in time and space and sharing the social and cultural predilections of that space and time. This is the central truth that literary history, following Bacon, keeps ever in view—a central truth that criticism neglects at its peril. We may with Holbrook Jackson write a book about the reader as artist, but we shall have to conclude as he concludes, by remarking that:

> Insulated art is decadent when it attempts to remove consciousness from the common stream of life which is as necessary to us as the blood stream to the body. Life is communalised experience and any attempt to side-track that experience to your own whim for seclusion, though bound in the end to fail, is theft or sabotage or both.[6]

Literary history as envisaged by Bacon is, then, the record of literature as communalized experience. As such it furnishes us with the necessary correlatives to criticism, which is forever subjective and private, whatever the pretensions of critical theory to objective truth, the enunciation of impersonal laws, or the establishment of standards of taste that have enduring and absolute value. For literary history, alas! is compelled to reveal that the history of taste is, among other things, a succession of abandoned absolutes.

Since it would be idle to discuss literary history in the abstract, I have settled upon the literary history of our own nation as my theme. I doubt if any part of modern letters gives us a more complicated or more exciting area to explore. This is true not because American literature is American and therefore of unique interest to us, but because we have as a nation been a huge laboratory experiment in the making of a national literature in modern times. A mature people, migrating, brought with them a mature literary tradition; yet such have been the shaping forces of environment, that this literature has developed characteristics of its own—perhaps more to be felt than to be particularized—which differentiate it from its origin, despite the truth that the vast resources of education, secondary and higher, have for years been thrown in the direction of maintaining British literary masterpieces as the norm of American taste.

We have produced every sort of literary history. We have had histories of American literature based upon racial theory, upon economic determinism, upon theories of the unconscious, upon political ideology, and upon moral idealism. We have had histories that embrace the whole nation, and we have had books devoted to particular regions only—New England, the Ohio Valley, the South—the novelty of which does not strike us until we conjure up the image of a literary history of Yorkshire or of the country south of the Thames. We have had books that deal with particular epochs and we have had histories of literary genres felt to be distinctively national, like the short story. Historians once argued that American literature is at best only a branch of English literature; and others have announced that the colloquial style of Artemus Ward, Mark Twain, Ring Lardner, and Will Rogers is the truly American thing, the prose of James Russell Lowell, George Edward Woodberry, and William Crary Brownell being alien, British, and treasonable to the American muse. The most influential book in the field—Parrington's *Main Currents in American Thought*—never purported to be a literary history; yet to some of our most penetrating literary histories the Americans pay no attention, for the reason that they are written by French and German scholars. In sum, a variety of contrasts charms and confuses the explorer of this trackless field.

## NOTES TO CHAPTER I

[1] "Tradition and the Individual Talent," in *The Sacred Wood* (London, 1928), p. 49. The whole passage is interesting and should be thoughtfully analyzed. Mr. Eliot argues, as I understand him, that no one can hope to be a poet beyond his twenty-fifth year except as he develops the historical sense ("tradition"); and he defines this historical sense as a simultaneous perception of the pastness of the past and of its projection into the present. One who has developed this historical sense will write "not merely with his own generation in his bones" but also with a feeling of (or for?) European literature from Homer to his own time, as also with a feeling of (or for?) his own national literature. For Mr. Eliot this literature (or these literatures) has "a simultaneous existence and composes a simultaneous order." (The word "simultaneous" has now somewhat shifted its meaning.) In other words, the historical sense, which is at the heart of "tradition," is a sense (a) of timelessness; (b) of the temporally past; (c) and of the temporally past and the temporally present as existing simultaneously.

This juggling is ingenious but induces in at least one reader an unseemly desire for logic. Waiving the problem of equating tradition with a historical sense which is simultaneously a sense of the past, a sense of the timeless, and a sense of the past, of timelessness, and of the present coexisting in a single moment, one is led to inquire why the work of an author written before twenty-five is thus inferentially cast out of the temporal order of literature either in his own country or in Europe, especially since this earlier work is likely to be imitative of past literatures to its own harm? Why twenty-five? Or twenty-one? Or any other age? And if the "pastness" of the past is now part of its "presence" (i.e., present experience, maturity, and knowledge), what guarantee can there be that the simultaneous order of a past thus experienced in a local present is necessarily identical with its real (i.e., temporally actual and permanently valuable) order? Obviously there can be no such guarantee. Yet if the historical order is not felt in present time, what *is* experienced can only be a local, subjective variant satisfying a local need for a usable past. That this is not merely an academic question may be shown by comparing the "European past" of Chaucer, of Pope, and

16

of Swinburne, so far as their several variants embrace the same names. Each of these famous poets thought of himself in some sense as a traditionalist, yet their "pasts" have little in common. Meanwhile, of course, the proposition that particular writers have had their imaginations enkindled by the thought and art of past epochs remains unassailable.

[2] Summarized from W. S. Holt, "The Idea of Scientific History in America," *Journal of the History of Ideas,* I(3), 352–362 (June, 1940). And for a more complete study of the ambiguities of "history" see *Theory and Practice in Historical Study: A Report of the Committee on Historiography* (New York: Social Science Research Council, n.d.), with its valuable bibliography.

[3] See his "Theory of Literary History," *Travaux du cercle linguistique de Prague,* VI, 173–191 (1936); "Periods and Movements in Literary History," *English Institute Annual* (New York, 1940), pp. 73–93; "Literary History," *Literary Scholarship: Its Aims and Methods,* ed. Norman Foerster (Chapel Hill, 1941), pp. 91–130; *Rise of English Literary History* (Chapel Hill, 1941).

[4] *The Works of Francis Bacon,* ed. Spedding, Ellis, and Heath, VIII (Boston, 1858), 419–420.

[5] Albert Guérard, *Literature and Society* (Boston, 1935), p. 3.

[6] Holbrook Jackson, *The Reading of Books* (New York, 1947), p. 267.

# II

# "Where Liberty Exalts the Mind"

THE STORY of American literature is, then, the record of a unique laboratory experiment. The general outlines of that story are of course familiar and may be found in all the books. English-speaking settlers arrive in North America, children of British intellectual and literary traditions. In the New World they and their descendants develop first a colonial, then a provincial, and finally a national, culture. In part the verbal expression of that culture, their literature grows with its growth, product of a particular physical and social environment, of new sentiments of nationalism and old reverence for what is inherited, of curiosity about the art and thought of continental Europe and eventually of Asia, and of cultural pressures from increasing numbers of racial groups, who, migrating later, finally outnumber the descendants of the pioneers, yet adopt their speech and their books while modifying both to new needs and new desires. This extraordinary transformation occupies less than three centuries and a half. Its result is a literature which has become one of the leading literatures of the globe, paying back with interest the cultures from which it borrowed. Here, surely, is a unique problem for the literary historian.

But though the history is familiar, we are without agreement as to the causes of this unparalleled development, perhaps the most remarkable in modern times. Theories are as plentiful as blackberries in August, and to an examination of some of these theories and of their history we shall by and by turn. We shall, however, better understand what the theoretical problem of American literature is by having clearly in mind what it is not; and I must therefore briefly discuss three or four leading presuppositions, methods, or hypotheses, important for the study of literary history, which either have seldom been advanced or clearly do not apply to the American problem. By so doing we shall hope to clarify the historical issues we are to face.

Inasmuch as modern philology in the broad sense was the product of romanticism, particularly of romantic German nationalism, histories of literature principally conditioned by nineteenth-century predilections, when they have sought the origins of a national letters, have commonly sought to educe them from the spirit of its language and from the earliest oral traditions of the nation. Thus historians of French literature mount up the stream of time to the Strasbourg oaths or even to ancient, if unliterary, Gaul; histories of English literature often begin with the genesis and development of the language from Anglo-Saxon times downward; and German literary historians since Herder have sometimes developed a racial mysticism grounded upon the supposed evidence of the Germanic spirit discoverable in language and folk literature. Thus also Professor Theodore Thienemann of the University of Pesth, at the International Congress of Literary History in 1931, divided all literary history into three vast epochs: a preliteral period of oral transmission, a period of manuscript, and the period of the book. So influential has been

19

the hypothesis that any national literature must begin with folk poetry that at the same congress Professor Alexander Eckhardt of Budapest pointed out, when the Czechs, the Hungarians, the Rumanians, and other central Europeans could discover no authentic preliteral material, they forged folk epics and folk legends as Macpherson forged his Ossianic poems to supply Scotland with a similar point of origin. This failure to distinguish what is popular from what is national shows how Herder was misunderstood.[1]

No such problem troubles American literary history. American literature sprang full-fledged from the brow of a British Jove. Our principal preliteral material is Amerindian, and though writers from Longfellow to La Farge have based imaginative work on Indian stories, it has never been pretended that aboriginal matter of this sort "created" American literature as the Anglo-Saxon tradition was supposed to carry English letters in its bosom. No oral tradition preceded Captain John Smith as the Homeric lays, if there were any, preceded the *Iliad*. And the fact that American literary history lies entirely within the third of Professor Thienemann's epochs—the period of the book—has meant that those who seek to define its qualities cannot or do not follow European example in this regard.

A second negation must be made. Histories of European literatures written after the philosophy of Hegel became influential sometimes read like textbooks in metaphysics. For example, here is a sentence from Rudolf Haym's book on German romanticism:

The world and its history may no longer be considered as a poem but as a methodical system, no longer as the creation of an absolute genius but as the teleologically determined development of an absolute and self-conscious spirit, a beautiful yet

20

fully comprehensible organism, the organism of reason and of intellectual reality.[2]

If one asks what this has to do with literary history, one must remember that a whole dialect of spirituality and historicity, periodization and unity, antithesis and polarity, came into being during the nineteenth century in order to force the arts into Hegelian form. And if Hegelianism no longer flourishes, modern scholars have created metaphysical systems of their own. In Russia and in Czechoslovakia we learn that literary history has developed a school of formalists who, avoiding the direct study of the intellectual and emotional content of literary works, analyze their phonemes; and, setting forth twelve principles for the guidance of literary history, the Rumanian savant, Michel Dragomirescu, declares that a masterpiece exists dually in a psychophysical world and possesses three distinct originalities—psychic, which is related to affective knowledge; plastic, which is related to intellectual knowledge; and harmonious, which is subjective-objective and is related to energetic knowledge.[3] My point is not merely that, however valuable these systems may prove to be, they are mostly unknown in the United States; my point is that the pragmatic nature of the American spirit has prevented us from regarding even transcendentalism as an aspect of the world soul taking on temporal form. American scholarship has not yet gone mystic or metaphysical.

We may also put aside a third hypothesis. When evolution was supposed to be the key to life and knowledge, Brunetière in France and John Addington Symonds in England argued that literary genres are subject to the law of evolution.[4] The one critic traced the evolution of tragedy from the Greeks through the Elizabethans to its modern decline; the other sought to derive French lyric poetry in the nineteenth century from the pulpit eloquence of the seventeenth. Other scholars have recorded the rise and fall of the Pindaric ode, of the sonnet sequence, and of pastoral romance on the supposition, expressed or implied, that literary forms evolve in life cycles comparable to zoological forms.

Although it would not be quite accurate to say that the theory of literary evolution has not interested American historians (all later historical writing is in some degree conditioned by the evolutionary hypothesis), the fact that there is no peculiar or characteristic American literary genre—not even the tall tale is wholly ours—has meant that American scholars have not found the evolutionary theory of literary forms particularly or peculiarly useful. There are, of course, books on the American short story, the American novel, the American drama, and the like, but these are descriptive rather than hypostatic; and if literary genres evolve, they usually evolve without special reference to the American scene. In sum, the whole problem of the development or decline of American letters has been studied without reference to this kind of evolutionary interpretation.

We might instance other theories that American scholarship ignores. Among the Germans, for example, the problem of what constitutes a literary generation and of the psychical relation among generations is hotly debated, whereas in the United States our only generation was a lost one and we have not concerned ourselves with the *Generationsproblem.*[5] What constitutes a literary age or period is also much debated abroad; we have solved the problem imperfectly and pragmatically without reference to principles, each historian making such divisions as he pleases or allowing them to be made for him by political events. And there are other theories. But it is perhaps time to turn to positive rather than negative aspects of the problem of American literary history.

2

We may begin our study by remarking the strong sense of history and of historic destiny which, from the beginning, has marked our development. America began as history; and a lasting tincture of the historical is in our blood. Not to labor the point that Columbus assumed he had found a continent wrinkled deep in time, we note that the creation of the English colonies was regarded by their makers as a unique historical event. The eyes of God, of the world, and of posterity were upon these experiments, sacred in New England, secular in Virginia. Wrote Captain John Smith:

*Columbus, Cortez, Pitzara, Soto, Magellanes,* and the rest serued more than a prentiship to learne how to begin their most memorable attempts in the *West Ind[i]es:* which to the wonder of all ages successfully they effected, when many hundreds of others, farre aboue them in the worlds opinion, beeing instructed but by relation, came to shame and confusion. . . .

Sharing the common view that the rise and fall of kingdoms are cyclical, Smith nevertheless called upon the English to create a new and virtuous empire:

What so truely su[i]ts with honour and honestie, as the discouering things vnknowne? erecting Townes, peopling Countries, informing the ignorant, reforming things vniust, teaching virtue; and . . . so farre from wronging any, as to cause Posteritie to remember thee; and remembring thee, euer honour that remembrance with praise.[6]

Posterity has wonderfully accommodated itself to this mandate, for Jamestown is now a public monument maintained by the government.

Bradford and Winthrop, two historians, stand at the head of New England literature and are followed by a regiment of recorders of remarkable providences. But remarkable providences are the stuff of history, so that half colonial literature is record, annals, history, apologia for significant action. Moreover, the controversial literature of the colonial period, whether it argue colony making or church government, paper money or taxation, is steeped in the historical point of view, appealing to precedent or ancient document, fateful judicial decision or life in the early church. A nation which creates the American Antiquarian Society only a few years after adopting a constitution is, indeed, historically minded; and today our road signs, our maps, our tourist books, our guides appeal to history in a degree that astonishes the European. We devote a series of volumes to rivers, another to historic lakes, a third to historical highways. In vain Emerson protests against this backward look, in vain Whitman denounces "feudal" habits of thought; we remain historically conscious, our leading newspaper demands national history be taught to all, the first success of our first complete man of letters is a burlesque of history, and the latest wonder in the publishing world is Toynbee's book on what history is all about. Whatever the explanation—whether it means that we self-consciously remind ourselves of what older regions take for granted, whether the role of this historical consciousness is to stabilize and unify our heterogeneous population, or whether we have confused a flattering sense of destiny with the history of the world—we cannot ignore this historical consciousness as a determinant in the na-tional mind.

3

Yet, despite this historical enthusiasm and although American literature is as old as Jamestown, no history of that subject appears until 1829. When we ask why this is so, we confront not only the general truth that literary history is everywhere a late development, but also a local situation of some complexity.

It may be said that there was no American literature worth a history in the seventeenth and eighteenth cen-turies. Certainly the seventeenth and eighteenth centuries are poor in literature written mainly to delight, but the mere listing of titles of books and pamphlets published in the future United States between 1639 and 1799 occupies twelve volumes of the Evans bibliography and runs to 35,854 items, so that there was a considerable body of printed material on which the literary historian could have exercised his skill. He did not appear, however; and the usual explanation is that the Americans were too busy with practical problems to trouble themselves about belles-lettres. The explanation does not explain. They were not too busy to establish seminaries of learning, to shape a theology, to lay the foundations of American science, and to produce that very library of theological and didactic works modern criticism finds dull. You can even find the rudiments of a literary theory in seventeenth-century New England and, more richly developed, in most of the colonies in the eighteenth century. But you do not find in the colonial period the beginnings of a literary history. What you have is merely the biographies of men who wrote.

In one way this is not astonishing. In another sense, however, since all the elements making for literary history were present—learning, a strong sense of historic mission, a feeling that the society involved is unique and important—it is surprising that when the colonies undertook so many kinds of historical writing, they did not also attempt literary history. But to do so the colonial scholar would have had to make two assumptions for which he was unprepared. The first was that English, the language of the market place and the forum, was a medium capable of elegant literature; the second was the possibility that geniuses could arise in America to rival those of Jerusalem, Athens, and Rome. Colonial learning, however, to the immense disgust of forward-looking Americans, persisted in clinging to Hebrew, Greek, and Latin. A sentence Edward Eggleston dug up from a *Life of Knox* exactly expresses this attitude: *Tres sunt linguae elegantes et ingenuae, Hebraica, Graeca, et Latina, quae nobilibus principibus sunt dignae:—ceteras linguas, cum sint barbarae,* barbaris *et* haereticis *tanquam propriis relinquo.* [7]

It is difficult for the atomic age vividly to grasp the supposed connection between the capacity of the governing classes to direct the state and the supposed benefits of the learned tongues, even though Hebrew silently disappeared from the discussion by the end of the eighteenth century. Yet the Boston Latin School, which proudly claims 1635 as its origin, numbered among its alumni in colonial times an important fraction of the governing classes in Massachusetts; perhaps for this reason the study of English composition was not introduced until 1823 and the study of English and American literature was postponed until 1870.[8] When in 1684 the Hopkins Grammar School was instituted in New Haven, the declared aim of the institution was this: "The Erection of ye said Schoole being principally for ye Institucion of hopeful youth in ye Latin tongue, and other learned Languages soe far as to prepare such youths for ye colledge and publique service of ye Country in Church, & Commonwealth." [9] If Franklin created his famous Academy as an "English" school because English was useful, the "College of Philadelphia" which grew out of the project in 1755, to become eventually the University of Pennsylvania, soon fell into the hands of the governing group (to Franklin's disappointment), with the interesting results that William Smith's plan of the curriculum (adopted in 1756) recommends the *Spectator, Rambler,* and other English readings for the student's "private hours," but builds courses around the learned tongues. Indeed, when the Continental Congress attended a Philadelphia commencement in May, 1775, they listened to a Latin oration and a Latin syllogistic dispute: *"Utrum detur sensus moralis"* [10]—a performance less disconcerting than it would have been to a contemporary congress, inasmuch as many of the founding fathers were formally educated in Latin, Greek, and scholastic philosophy.[11] And by the end of the eighteenth century conservative horror at the excesses of the revolutionary spirit had led to a conservative reaffirmation of the special values of Latin and Greek— a fact that may easily be illustrated. In 1799 the Rev. Samuel Knox published at Baltimore *An Essay on the Best System of Liberal Education, Adapted to the Genius of the Government of the United States.* This little book was compounded of an address to the Maryland legislature, in part responsible for shaping Washington College in that state, and of an essay which had won the prize of the American Philosophical Society for a discussion of "the best System of liberal Education and literary instruction" suitable to the United States. The Rev. Mr. Knox looked with scorn on the prevailing "false taste in education," content with "a smattering of French, arithmetic, and those branches connected with it," which makes learning a mere "handmaid to industry"; and, opposing this "vitiated taste," he stoutly demanded a return to the "solid and invaluable advantages" of Greek and Latin because, since

most of the sciences and especially their elements were originally written in the Greek or Roman languages, it must certainly tend to assist and enlighten the mind of the learner to be acquainted radically with the technical terms of that art; or the principles of that science which is the subject of his study.

Only such studies "aim at the highest improvement of the mind"; and the good man denies Dr. Rush's opinion that "the acquisition of the Greek and Latin languages; the minutiae of their grammars; and a well formed taste for the beauties of the ancient classical writers, has a tendency to damp natural genius. . . ." On the contrary, let the governing classes start their children early at Latin; let them return to that "classical erudition, a few years since so liberally patronised by many in the most polished places in Maryland." [12]

Against this hidebound conservatism two attacks were launched, often indistinguishable from each other. On the one hand, practical-minded Americans found a medieval education useless in a New World; on the other, struggling writers wanted support and an audience that a learned curriculum could not supply. As it is often difficult to disentangle the arguments of the practical from the efforts of American writers to force the learned class to recognize a special worth in English literature written in the future United States, one can here do little more than quote representative opinions, many of which combine both views. Thus, discussing the education of the sons of planters, Hugh Jones, in *The Present State of Virginia* (1724), roundly said they would be better trained if they had stuck to English: "In *English* may be conveyed to them (without going directly to *Rome* and *Athens*) all the Arts, Sciences, and learned Accomplishments of the Antients and Moderns without the Fatigue and Expence of another Language for which few of them have little Use or Necessity." [13] Outlining an educational Utopia in his *General Idea of the College of Mirania* in 1753, the Rev. William Smith (who blew hot and cold with respect to the classic languages) lamented there was "no collegiate School for breeding Mechanics" and set up on paper a curriculum for them which expressly omitted the learned tongues. Even for the children of the gentry he seems to have preferred English, since English is most apt for declamation, oratory, and poetry, that "eldest daughter of Eloquence." Why, then, neglect one's native language? The ladies will not understand Latin declamations, whereas English oratory and declamation

enlarge the Mind, refine and exalt the Understanding, improve the Temper, soften the Manners, serve the Passions, cherish Reflection, and lead on that charming Languor of the Soul, that philosophic Melancholy, which, most of all disposes to Love, Friendship, and every tender Emotion.[14]

The practical analogue of the College of Mirania was, of course, Franklin's extremely unclassical academy in Philadelphia. The quarrel between Franklin and Smith rose partly out of political considerations, partly out of Franklin's profound distrust of a classical education administered by and for gentlemen; and writing his "Observations Relative to the Intentions of the Original Founders of the Academy in Philadelphia," Franklin compared the usefulness of Latin and Greek in America to the *chapeau bras*— a hat carried under the arm by a fop but never put on his head. "The utility," he dryly remarked, "of such a mode of wearing it is by no means apparent, and it is attended not only with some expense, but with a degree of constant trouble." [15]

Despite his own classical predilections, evident in his poem, "Philosophic Solitude," in which he invites a number of friends to share an American Sabine farm with him, William Livingston declared against the ancient languages as the staple of American education. Writing to the Bishop of Llandaff in 1768, he said:

We want hands, my lord, more than heads. The most intimate acquaintance with the classics, will not remove our oaks; nor a taste for the *Georgics* cultivate our lands. Many of our young people are knocking their heads against the *Iliad,* who should employ their hands in clearing our swamps, and draining our marshes.[16]

Nor is the attack to be interpreted as crass vocationalism. Eulogizing David Rittenhouse, Dr. Benjamin Rush thought it an excellent thing that the astronomer had escaped

the pernicious influence of monkish learning upon his mind in early life. Had the usual forms of a public education in the United States been imposed upon him, instead of revolving through life in a planetary orbit, he would probably have consumed the forces of his genius . . . in composing syllogisms, or in measuring the feet of Greek and Latin poetry.[17]

And two frontal assaults upon the conservative position toward the end of the century are too characteristic to be ignored.

The reader of the *Miscellaneous Essays and Occasional Writings of Francis Hopkinson* (1792) soon discovers that this Revolutionary wit had small patience with the conservative order in the colleges. The opening essay in his first volume is a dream allegory in which scholastic logic is compared to a swamp; and the second ridicules Latin, logic, and the scholastic form of "natural philosophy" by suggesting these be taught to children in the form of hopscotch. The most amusing of Hopkinson's satires are undoubtedly the ones entitled "Modern Learning: Exemplified by a Specimen of a Collegiate Examination"—in which the properties and accidents of a common salt box are gravely analyzed according to current academic notions—and, in the second volume, a series of "Orations, written for, and at the request of young gentlemen of the university, and delivered by them at public commencements in the college hall," which mercilessly pillories Latin and its accompanying philosophy as a principal enemy of American literature:

Through this grammar . . . the bewildered pupil must wade, groping for a year or two in utter darkness, and learning by rote a complicated system of rules, the propriety or application of which it is impossible for him to see in any instance.

The first observable consequence is, that he loses, or at least gains, no ground in a taste for the elegancies of his native tongue. His diction becomes stiff and awkward, and his hand writing intolerable. So that whilst he is studying the anatomy of

31

a dead language, he remains a stranger to the beauties of the living.

A brace of orations "on the learned languages" argues that there is no inherent magic in them to polish manners, that, if antiquity is their defense, the study of Chinese should be even more valuable, that they are no longer a medium of general communication, and that they corrupt style by inducing a flow of high-sounding words.[18]

If such were the views of a brilliant young Pennsylvanian, similar views were expressed by an equally brilliant young writer in Connecticut. The preface to Trumbull's *Progress of Dulness,* parts one and two, explicitly declares that the author's purpose is to show in 1772 that

the mere knowledge of the ancient languages, of the abstruser parts of mathematics, and the dark researches of metaphysics, is of little advantage in any business or profession in life;—that it would be more beneficial, in every place of public education, to take pains in teaching the elements of oratory, the grammar of the English tongue, and the elegancies of style and composition.

In the poem itself Tom Brainless, after a dull preparatory education shaped by Lily's Latin grammar, a Latin Testament, Virgil, Cicero, and a Greek lexicon, goes to college only to find academic studies equally pointless; and Trumbull comments:

> how oft the studious gain,
> The dulness of a letter'd brain;
> Despising such low things the while,
> As English grammar, phrase and style;
> Despising ev'ry nicer art,
> That aids the tongue, or mends the heart;
>
> .     .     .     .     .

> And plodding on in one dull tone,
> Gain ancient tongues and lose their own.

Eventually the poet implores learning to come out of the library into the sunlight of contemporary life:

> Oh! might I live to see that day
> When sense shall point to youths their way.
>
> .    .    .    .    .
>
> Give ancient arts their real due,
> Explain their faults, and beauties too.
>
> .    .    .    .    .
>
> Our youths might learn each nobler art,
> That shews a passage to the heart;
> From ancient languages well known
> Transfuse new beauties to our own;
> With taste and fancy well refin'd,
> Where moral rapture warms the mind,
> From schools dismiss'd, with lib'ral hand,
> Spread useful learning o'er the land;
> And bid the eastern world admire
> Our rising worth, and brightn'ing fire.[19]

But despite these blameless couplets, American scholarship continued its refusal to recognize the American muse; and the general reaction to the French Revolution temporarily strengthened the hands of educational conservatives.

## 4

The American muse, however, insisted upon recognition, and not only upon that, but upon recognition as something novel, unique, unprecedented, and different from anything Europe could possibly produce. You cannot blame her for being pert. She had the blessing of the Anglican church. Bishop Berkeley had written:

> The muse, disgusted at an age and clime
> Barren of every glorious theme,
> In distant lands now waits a better time,
> Producing subjects worthy fame.

> . . . .

> There, shall be sung another golden age,
> The rise of empire and of arts;
> The good and great, inspiring epick rage;
> The wisest heads and noblest hearts.

> Not such as Europe breeds, in her decay,
> Such as she bred, when fresh and young;
> When heavenly flame did animate her clay,
> By future poets shall be sung.

> Westward the star of empire takes its way. . . .

The westering star of empire implied the birth of a fresh and novel literary art.

Thus, in the middle of the eighteenth century, Nathaniel Evans invited the muse to settle on the banks of the Schuylkill River:

> Where liberty exalts the mind;
> Where plenty basks the live long day,
> And pours her treasures unconfin'd.
> Hither ye beauteous *virgins* tend,
> With *Arts* and *Science* by your side,
> Whose skill th'untutor'd morals mend,
> And to fair honour mankind guide; [20]

but it soon appeared that the arts and sciences were to descend from heaven, not emigrate from Europe. Said a writer in the *American Whig* in 1768:

The benefits we enjoy from our situation, our climates, and the fecundity of the soil are numberless, and not to be recounted. No quarter of the globe can boast a preheminence: No nation in some respects pretend to an equality. . . . Never was there such a *Phoenix state*. . . . Courage, then, Americans! liberty, religion and sciences are on the wing to these shores! The finger of God points out a mighty empire to your sons. . . .[21]

The Rev. Jacob Duché, once famous as the author of *Caspipina's Letters*, developed the theme even more richly in 1774:

In Europe the several arts and sciences are almost arrived at their meridian of perfection; at least, new discoveries are less frequent now than heretofore. . . . The eye is weary with a repetition of scenes, in which it discovers a perpetual sameness, though heightened by all the refinements of taste. . . . [But] the objects of art, as well as those of nature, in this new world, are at present in such a state, as affords the highest entertainment to these faculties of the mind. The progression is begun: Here and there, in the midst of venerable woods, which, scarce a century ago, were the uncultivated haunts of roaming savages, the power of cultivation presents itself to the travellers view, in opening lawns, covered with the richest verdure, fields of corn, orchards, gardens, and meadows fertilized by well-directed streams—Hamlets, villages, and even populous cities, with their towering spires, excite our admiration. . . . The progress of the human mind may here likewise be observed to keep equal pace with the external improvements.

In proof of intellectual progress he affirmed that

literary accomplishments here meet with deserved applause. But such is the prevailing taste for books of every kind, that almost every man is a reader; and by pronouncing sentence, right or wrong, upon the various publications that come in his way, puts himself upon a level, in point of knowledge, with their several authors.[22]

Since, as Nathaniel Ames, Jr., the almanac maker, had written, a new Locke and Milton, an American Newton and Shakespeare were to arise on "Ontario's shore"; [23] since in Great Britain, according to Isaiah Thomas, literary fame was declining, and it was "reserved for this new world to produce those noble works of genius to which past ages can afford nothing parallel," [24] the democratic inference was irresistible that the Americans had passed beyond decaying monarchical cultures whence a conservative scholarship derived.

And in fact this inference becomes the theme song, as it were, of a whole new literary generation at the end of the eighteenth century. When Messrs. Dwight and Barlow, just before the Revolution, were meditating a London publication of their poems, Trumbull poetically entreated them not to be put down by British criticism but to

> Prove to the world, in these new-dawning skies,
> What genius kindles and what arts arise;
> What fav'ring Muses lent their willing aid
>
> .    .    .    .    .
>
> While in your strains the purest morals flow'd,
> Rules to the great, and lessons to the good.
>
> .    .    .    .    .
>
> Fame shall assent, and future years admire
> Barlow's strong flight, and Dwight's Homeric fire.[25]

It was an idea Trumbull had earlier presented to Yale, where in 1770 he had called on American poetry to

> wake from nature's themes the moral song,
> And shine with Pope and Thompson and with Young.
> This land her Swift and Addison shall view,
> The former honours equall'd by the new;
> Here shall some Shakespeare charm the rising age,
> And hold in magic chains the listening stage;
> A second Watts shall string the heavenly lyre,
> And other muses other bards inspire.[26]

When Colonel Humphreys planned to depart for Europe in 1785, Timothy Dwight entreated him to be careful. In Europe, unfortunately, "To brothels, half the female world is driven"; and his brother reformer feared the colonel might there forget America, "where Trumbull leads the ardent throng," and where poets are to "fill with worth the part assign'd by Heaven." [27] In Barlow's own *Columbiad*, which began life as *The Vision of Columbus* in 1787, the Connecticut Mutual Admiration Society made its canonical appearance toward the end of Book VIII, where Trumbull, Dwight, and Humphreys are hailed by name and we learn of American poetry:

> To equal fame ascends thy tuneful throng,
> The boast of genius and the pride of song;
> Caught from the cast of every age and clime,
> Their lays shall triumph o'er the lapse of time,

and the connection with the anticlassical, anti-European doctrine of the group is clear from the vision of universal peace in Book X:

> No foreign terms shall crowd with barbarous rules
> The dull unmeaning pageantry of schools;
> Nor dark authorities nor names unknown
> Fill the learn'd head with ignorance not its own;
> But wisdom's eye with beams unclouded shine,
> And simplest rules her native charms define;
> One living language, one unborrow'd dress
> Her boldest flights with fullest force express.[28]

The Connecticut wits, despairing of collegiate conservatism, announced that Europe was done for and that the hope of literature no longer lay with the dead languages.

In that strange poem, *Greenfield Hill* (1794), a series of

imitations of British bards, Timothy Dwight employed a succession of borrowed styles to proclaim that American life, letters, and learning were to flee out of Europe:

> Ah, then, thou favour'd land, thyself revere!
> Look not to Europe, for examples just
> Of order, manners, customs, doctrines, laws,
> Of happiness, or virtue. Cast around
> The eye of searching reason, and declare
> What Europe proffers, but a patchwork sway.
>
> .    .    .    .    .
>
> Change, but change alone,
> By wise improvement of thy blessings rare;
> And copy not from others. Shun the lures
> Of Europe.

And after an excited picture of American commerce courting "Korean gales," of Indians transformed by the "gospel's sunshine" and of marshes turned into golden meadows, Dwight prophesied that

> Where slept perennial night, shall science rise,
> And new-born Oxfords cheer the evening skies;
> Miltonic strains the Mexic hills prolong
> And Louis murmurs to Sicilian song.[29]

We shall have to forgive him such Briticisms as "Oxford" and "Milton," inasmuch as the national language was still English. But his intent was like that of Humphreys, who, addressing American poets, bade

> bards melodious charm the listening throng,
> Thrill'd with the raptures of ecstatic song,[30]

only it was to be a new song because progress was progress despite the academic mind, and republican virtue could not possibly copy monarchical forms.

Indeed, it is curious to find these poets, most of them

conservative, obeying Thomas Jefferson's command to avoid Europe. The fever overran the imagination of the country like a contagion. Perhaps the greatest single source of infection was Noah Webster, whose blue-black speller demanded an American orthography and whose *Grammatical Institute of the English Language, Part III* (1785) became in 1787 *An American Selection of Lessons in Reading and Speaking, Calculated to Improve the Minds and Refine the Taste of Youth, and also to Instruct them in Geography, History, and Politics of the United States,* which went through innumerable printings to 1816. The preface demanded a purely American literature:

> Europe is grown old in folly, corruption, and tyranny. In that country laws are perverted, manners are licentious, literature is declining, and human nature is debased. . . . American glory begins to dawn at a favorable period, and under flattering circumstances. We have the experience of the whole world before our eyes; but to receive indiscriminately the maxims of government, the manners and literary taste of Europe, and make them the ground on which to build our systems in America, must soon convince us that a durable and stately edifice can never be erected upon the mouldering pillars of antiquity.[31]

It was in vain for conservatives to protest, as did the Rev. Thaddeus Brown in 1798, that modern books unblessed by the colleges induce "disobedience to parents—debaucheries—prostitutions—broken promises—perjuries—adulteries—suicides and other crimes too horrid to name . . . caused by learning in, and inculcated from this abominable library of hell"; [32] or for David Daggett, in a pamphlet picturesquely entitled *Sun-Beams may be Extracted from Cucumbers, but the Process is Tedious,* ironically to defend conservative academic wisdom:

We all recollect when these principles began to impress our Colleges—when it was seriously contended that the study of mathematics and natural philosophy was ruinous to the health, genius and character of a young gentleman . . . and that Latin and Greek were fitted only for stupid divines or black-letter lawyers; [33]

or for William Dunlap to declare, as he did, that the state of American literature was "extremely superficial." Robert Bolling was proclaimed by a writer in the *Columbian Magazine* in 1788 "one of the greatest poetical geniuses that ever existed," and the American William Billings was rated by the same magazine as the rival of Handel.[34] A strange fusion of orthodoxy and radicalism prevailed. As Professor Leon Howard puts it, a

curious union between a complacent belief in the westward course of empire and an orthodox belief in the biblical millennium gave the minds of many Americans, especially New Englanders, a bias toward any general theories of progress that might explain the improvement they themselves had witnessed in the Colonies,[35]

and the American Revolution provided the emotional impulse further to drive them on. Whatever the conservatives might say, the future seemed to lie with the exuberance of poetry:

> I see, I see
> Freedom's established reign; cities, and men,
> Numerous as sands upon the ocean shore,
> And empires rising where the sun descends!—
> The *Ohio* soon shall glide by many a town
> Of note; and where the *Mississippi* stream,
> By forests shaded, now runs weeping on,
> Nations shall grow, and states not less in fame
> Than Greece and Rome of old! [36]

40

This calm appropriation of the classic world by bellicose young America reminds one of the national political apothegm: "If you can't lick them, join them."

By the end of the eighteenth century collegiate learning had lost its opportunity to guide the development of American literature. It had clung to conservatism; and the split between scholarship and writing steadily widened. Modernists flung the usefulness of the English language into the faces of learned men still doggedly proclaiming the virtues of Hebrew, Greek, and Latin; and now that a new nation had come into being, modernists further insisted that the national literature was to have few or no historic roots, was to be a novel culture in a novel commonwealth, was to replace classic letters as radically as, in the Soviet Republic, revolutionary writing is supposed to replace a bourgeois literature.[37]

Clearly there could be no history of American literature when American literature thus proclaimed itself unhistorical. The national letters, so far as educational interest was concerned, were principally consigned to the school readers—Webster, Bingham, Pierpont, Cobb, Swan, Town, Towers, Sanders, and eventually McGuffey, which, as *The American Preceptor* (1794) boasted, gave preference "to the productions of American genius," [38] whatever the colleges might do. Learning, which had founded Harvard, William and Mary, Yale, Columbia, and Princeton would therefore have little to do with this dangerous novelty until 1872, when Professor John S. Hart taught at Princeton the first collegiate course in American literature.[39] The paradox developed that a nation consciously steeping itself in a sense of historic mission consciously pretended for a period that its literature needed no historians and had no historic roots!

## NOTES TO CHAPTER II

[1] The record of this conference may be found in the *Bulletin of the International Committee of Historical Sciences,* No. 14, vol. IV, pt. 1 (February, 1932).

[2] Almost the penultimate sentence in Rudolf Haym, *Die romantische Schule: Ein Beitrag zur Geschichte des deutschen Geistes* (4th ed.; Berlin, 1920), p. 928.

[3] See his essay in the *Bulletin of the International Committee of Historical Sciences, op. cit.,* "Nouveau point de vue dans l'étude de la littérature."

[4] For Brunetière, see his *L'Evolution de genres dans l'histoire de la littérature* (Paris, 1890); for John Addington Symonds, "On the Application of Evolutionary Principles to Art and Literature" in *Essays Speculative and Suggestive* (2 vols.; London, 1890), I, 42–83.

[5] For a survey of German theory, highly speculative and some of it unintelligible, see the essays collected by E. Ermatinger, *Philosophie der Literaturwissenschaft* (Berlin, 1930).

[6] From *A Description of New England* (1616), in *Travels and Works of Captain John Smith,* ed. Arber and Bradley (2 vols.; Edinburgh, 1910), I, 191, 208–209.

[7] Eggleston misprinted the Latin. For the original reference see Thomas M'Crie, *The Life of John Knox* (New York, 1813), p. 472.

[8] See Pauline Holmes, *A Tercentenary History of the Boston Public Latin School, 1635–1935* (Cambridge, 1935), pp. 367–368.

[9] Quoted in E. D. Grizzell, *Origin and Development of the High School in New England before 1865* (Philadelphia, 1922), p. 11. This writer notes that the Latin school ended its major phase with the decline of the theocracy and the rise of merchants and tradesmen as well as the movement toward the frontier. It is an amusing instance of persisting snobbery that when in 1820 the Boston School Committee voted to establish an "English Classical School," they were compelled to rename it in 1824 the "English High School" (p. 42).

[10] Horace Wemyss Smith, *Life and Correspondence of the Rev. William Smith, D.D.* (2 vols.; Philadelphia, 1879), I, 54–59, 124, 500–501.

[11] See Rev. James J. Walsh, *Education of the Founding Fathers of the Republic: Scholasticism in the Colonial Colleges* (New York, 1935). Father Walsh believes that signers of the Declaration of Independence, if they went to college at all, were normally able to talk Latin at fourteen or fifteen.

[12] Rev. Samuel Knox, *An Essay on the Best System of Liberal Education, Adapted to the Genius of the Government of the United States* (Baltimore, 1799), pp. 17, 21, 45, 57–58.

[13] Hugh Jones, *The Present State of Virginia* (London, 1724), p. 46. "*Grammar* Learning [i.e., Latin grammar] taught after the common round-about Way is not much beneficial nor delightful to them . . . because they are imprisoned and enslaved to what they hate, and think useless." An appendix sketches a project for reforming William and Mary College, "a College without a Chapel, without a Scholarship, and without a Statute. There is a Library without Books, comparatively speaking, and a President without a fix'd Salary till of late"; and Jones wants a curriculum which will turn out "compleat Gentlemen and good Christians, and qualified for the Study of the Gospel, Law, or Physick; and prepared for undertaking Trade, or any useful Projects and Inventions" (p. 87).

[14] William Smith, *A General Idea of the College of Mirania* (New York, 1753), pp. 15–18, 25. We are not, the dialogue argues, to "wilder ourselves in the Search of Truth, among the Rubbish contain'd in the vast Tomes of ancient Rabbies, Commentators and Schoolmen" (p. 11); and declamations, public acts, and the like are to be in English, since "the Practice of neglecting the Mother-Tongue, and embarrassing a young Student, by obliging him to speak or compose in a dead Language" is to be condemned (pp. 36–37). Similar doctrine is expressed in the account of the founding of the Academy, reprinted in the *Life and Correspondence* already cited, vol. I, pp. 54–55, where one reads it would be "inexcusable" to neglect English; but five or six years later Smith, as we have seen, relegated English to the student's "private hours."

[15] *Writings of Benjamin Franklin*, ed. A. H. Smyth (10 vols.; New York, 1907), X, 9–31, especially pp. 29–31; and cf. Francis Newton Thorpe, "Franklin's Influence in American Education," *U.S. Bureau of Education: Report of the Commissioner of Education for 1902* (2 vols.; Washington, 1903), vol. I, chap. 2.

[16] *A Letter to the Right Reverend Father in God, John, Lord Bishop of Landaff* (New York, 1768). Livingston deeply resented the bishop's reference to the Americans as adventurers, "who, with

their native soil, abandoned their native manners and religion; and e'er [*sic*] long were found in many parts without remembrance or knowledge of God, without any divine worship, in dissolute wickedness, and the most brutal profligacy of manners." The bishop demanded more seminaries for ministers; Livingston retorted that "the most judicious among us, think our public seminaries *superfluously multiplied*" but defended practical education in the colleges. For his "Philosophic Solitude" see *American Poems, Selected and Original,* vol. I [*sic*] (Litchfield, 1793). There are extracts in Kettell.

[17] Benjamin Rush, *An Eulogium Intended to perpetuate the memory of David Rittenhouse, late President of the American Philosophical Society* (Philadelphia, 1797), pp. 23–24. Samuel Knox's dislike of Rush's educational theory in part inspired his essay on education already quoted.

[18] *Miscellaneous Essays and Occasional Writings of Francis Hopkinson, Esq.* (3 vols.; Philadelphia, 1792). Most of the miscellaneous essays in Volume I were originally published in the *Pennsylvania Magazine* during the middle seventies. The Harvard College copy of Volume II, containing the orations, in a series of penciled notes assigns dates and names for the delivery of the speeches.

[19] *Poetical Works of John Trumbull, LL.D., The Colonnade,* vol. XIV, 1919–1922 (The Andiron Club of New York, 1922), part 2. The quotations in the text may be found on pp. 413, 417, 421. After teaching school Brainless later studies under a preacher, where he learns to "torture words in thousand senses" and to "shun with anxious care, the while,/The infection of a modern style" (p. 424). On the other hand, in part two of the poem Dick Hairbrain is satirized because he learns only empty French phrases and other fopperies at college.

[20] See *Poems on Several Occasions* (Philadelphia, 1772), "Ode on the Prospect of Peace" (1761), especially pp. 28–29. Toward the end of the poem one reads:

> To such, may Delaware, majestic flood,
> Lend, from his flowery banks, a ravish'd ear;
> Such note as may delight the wise and good,
> Or saints celestial may endure to hear!
> For if the muse can aught of time descry,
> Such notes shall sound thy crystal waves along,
> Thy cities fair with glorious Athens vie,
> Nor pure Ilissus boast a nobler song.

On thy fair banks, a fane to Virtue's name
Shall rise—and justice light her holy flame.

This is an early and interesting instance of the amalgamation of American literary production with Christian virtue.

[21] *A Collection of Tracts from the Late News Papers, etc. Containing particularly The American Whig, A Whip for the American Whig, with some other pieces* (New York, 1768). The twentieth item in the collection is a reprint of the *American Whig* for April 11, 1768, from which the quotation in the text is taken.

[22] [Jacob Duché], *Observations on a Variety of Subjects, Literary, Moral and Religious; in a series of original letters, written by a Gentleman of Foreign Extraction* (Philadelphia, 1774), pp. 104–106, 30.

[23] *Essays, Humor and Poems of Nathaniel Ames*, ed. S. Briggs (Cleveland, 1891), under "1769."

[24] In the *Royal American Magazine* for 1774. On the significance of this periodical and for a study of the drive toward nationalism in early American periodicals, see Lyon N. Richardson's magisterial work, *A History of Early American Magazines* (New York, 1931).

[25] *Poetical Works*, ed. cit., p. 473. (Many of the passages quoted in the text can also be conveniently found in Vernon L. Parrington, *The Connecticut Wits*, New York, 1926.)

[26] *Ibid.*, p. 497.

[27] From his epistle to Humphreys in *American Poems, Selected and Original, op. cit.*, pp. 81, 83.

[28] Joel Barlow, *The Columbiad: A Poem* (Washington, 1825), pp. 293, 553–554. Note the amusing survey of American education:

To nurse the arts and fashion freedom's lore
Young schools of science rise along the shore;
Great without pomp their modest walls expand,
Harvard and Yale and Princeton grace the land;
Penn's student halls his youth with gladness greet,
On James's banks Virginia Muses meet,
Manhattan's mart colleagiate [*sic*] domes command,
Bosom'd in groves, see growing Dartmouth stand,
Bright o'er its realm reflecting solar fires,
On yon tall hill Rhode Island's seat aspires.

[29] Timothy Dwight, *Greenfield Hill: A Poem* (New York, 1794), pp. 18, 19, 52; and cf. p. 163.

[30] David Humphreys, *Miscellaneous Works* (New York, 1804), p. 113. Both his "Address to the Armies of the United States" and the better-known "Poem on the Happiness of America" rise to se-

raphic prophecy, but the "Poem on the Industry of the United States of America," quoted in the text, is more specific.

[31] For the bibliography of the Webster textbooks consult Ervin C. Shoemaker, *Noah Webster: Pioneer of Learning* (New York, 1936); and for the intellectual context of Webster's nationalism see Herbert W. Schneider, *A History of American Philosophy* (New York, 1946), pp. 100 ff.

[32] Thaddeus Brown, *An Address in Christian Love, to the Inhabitants of Philadelphia* (Philadelphia, 1798), pp. 49–50.

[33] David Daggett, *Sun-Beams may be Extracted from Cucumbers, but the Process is Tedious* (New Haven, 1799), p. 12. The oration is a rousing attack on French "infidelity," and conservatives generally equated literary modernity with the revolutionary spirit.

[34] Philadelphia *Universal Asylum, and Columbian Magazine* (April, 1788), vol. II, pt. 1, "Account of two Americans of extraordinary genius," pp. 211–213. Nature made Billings "just such a musician, as she made Shakespeare a poet" (p. 212).

[35] Leon Howard, *The Connecticut Wits* (Chicago, 1943), p. 151.

[36] From "The Rising Glory in America," which can be conveniently found in the *Poems of Freneau,* ed. Harry H. Clark (New York, 1929), p. 13. Hugh H. Breckenridge was also concerned in writing this poem.

[37] The theoretical novelty of American writing is implicit in the frequent appearance of "Columbian" or "American" in the titles of magazines of the period.

[38] On American readers down to about 1880 see Rudolph R. Reeder, *The Historical Development of School Readers and Method in Teaching Reading* (Columbia dissertation; New York, 1909). *The American Preceptor* by Bingham had reached sixty-four editions by 1832. Cobb's *North American Reader,* edition of 1835, is heavily patriotic and anti-British: "The pieces in this work are chiefly American. The English Reader [of Lindley Murray], the book most generally used in the schools of our country, does not contain a single piece or paragraph written by an American citizen. Is this good policy? Is it patriotism? Shall the children of this great nation be compelled to read, year after year, none but the writings and speeches of men whose views and feelings are in direct opposition to our institutions and government? . . . The United States have political and civil institutions of their own; and how can these be upheld unless the children and youth of our country are early made to understand them by books and other means of instruction?" (in Reeder, pp. 48–

49). By 1844 more than six million of Cobb's readers had been sold. By 1880 the sales of Webster had reached eighty million copies. On McGuffey see Harvey C. Minnich, *William Holmes McGuffey and His Readers* (New York, 1936); and Richard D. Mosier, *Making the American Mind: Social and Moral Ideas in the McGuffey Readers* (New York, 1947).

[39] Institutional pride has disputed the priority of Princeton in this regard, but pending the settlement of the controversy I give the usual date.

# III

# "A National Spirit in Letters"

T HE MOST FAMOUS PARAGRAPH in Crèvecoeur's *Letters of an American Farmer* contains
the rhetorical question: "What, then, is the
American, this new man?" Having recited the decisive effect of climate and institutions upon European immigrants
to the New World, Crèvecoeur declared:

> *He* is an American, who, leaving behind him all his ancient
> prejudices and manners, receives new ones from the new mode
> of life he has embraced, the new government he obeys, and the
> new rank he holds. . . . Americans are the western pilgrims,
> who are carrying along with them that great mass of arts, sci-
> ences, vigour, and industry which began long since in the east;
> they will finish the great circle.

In short, the American is "a new man, who acts upon new
principles; he must therefore entertain new ideas, and form
new opinions." What Crèvecoeur does not expressly state,
but what he might well have added is: The American reads
new books written by new authors in a new style notable
for not being European.[1] If there were no such books, it
was at any rate the revolutionary hope that the young republic would instantly produce a cultural Golden Age.

There were, of course, practical difficulties. In 1785 Jefferson might warn his correspondent against not only the

"voluptuary dress and arts of the European women" but also the "ruin" of "speaking and writing his native tongue as a foreigner" "unqualified to obtain those distinctions, which eloquence of the pen and tongue ensures in a free country": he might prophesy in 1813 that "should the language of England continue stationary, we shall probably enlarge our employment of it, until its new character may separate it in name as well as in power from the mother-tongue," but the sagacious philosopher was aware that literary culture is a slow growth: "Literature is not yet a distinct profession with us. Now and then a strong mind arises, and at its intervals of leisure from business, emits a flash of light. But the first object of young societies is bread and covering; science is but secondary and subsequent." [2] If Jefferson acquiesced in the poverty of the American Muse, others, among them many of his political opponents, desired few or no innovations.

In Federalist circles, including men of the type of Robert Treat Paine, Jr., Joseph Dennie, and young John Quincy Adams, literary conservatism was common. Some of them continued to write as if Pope and Churchill were regnant in the American heavens. The reader of the *Works in Verse and Prose, of the late Robert Treat Paine, Jun. Esq.,* if he passes over a few geographical references, occasional poems with local allusions, and a random passage or two, would never guess that these effusions were not London products. A passage in "The Ruling Passion" (1797) indicates that Pope was Paine's literary ideal:

> All hail, sweet Poesy! transcendent maid!
> To whom my fond youth's earliest vows were paid;
> Who, dressed in sapphire robes, with eye of fire,
> Didst first my unambitious rhyme inspire;

49

Lured by whose charms, I left, in passioned hope,
My Watts's Logick for the page of Pope;

and even the "Prize Prologue" for the opening of the first
Boston theater never got beyond a review of the leading
British dramatists, and a cautious hope that Sophocles,
Terence, and Sheridan would reign in Massachusetts:

Thy classick lares shall exalt our times,
With distant ages and remotest climes.[3]

As for Joseph Dennie—whom Tom Moore, then in his
Tory phase, found one of the few agreeable literary men in
America—despite some inconsistency and despite a genuine desire for American literature, his taste remained generally conservative, his biographer remarking that Dennie
accepted "the only safe standards he knew, those of eighteenth century England." [4] And though John Quincy Adams
translated Wieland's *Oberon* and imitated Byron, he repudiated most modern literature, for his taste was anchored
in the Bible, Cicero, Horace, Shakespeare, and certain
standard British authors of the seventeenth and eighteenth
centuries; and his Boylston lectures on rhetoric and oratory
(he was the first incumbent of that famous Harvard chair),
faithful to the statutes (which were in turn faithful to an
article on oratory in the *Encyclopaedia Britannica,* third
edition, Edinburgh, 1797), are solid expositions of the
classical theories of antiquity with only such modern ap-
peals for "pure English" as seemed necessary for clearness.
The existence of a school of American orators would
scarcely be suspected from these ponderous pages, just as
one would never learn from the published diary of the Old
Man Eloquent that writers like Hawthorne, Holmes, Longfellow, Lowell, or Whittier were at work. But a lengthy and

admiring analysis of the lectures, in the eighth volume of the *Monthly Anthology and Boston Review,* shows how greatly this conservatism appealed to Boston literati in 1810.[5] Perhaps one of the queerest bits of logic emanating from this group is found in a brace of articles by Walter Channing, published in the *North American Review* in 1815. This author admitted that "the whole elements of our literature, were they collected into one mass, would amount merely to accidental efforts of a very few adventurous individuals." He rather hopelessly surmised that since the country "possesses the same language with a nation, totally unlike it in almost every relation, . . . [it] delights more in the acquisition of foreign literature, than in a laborious independent exertion of its own intellectual powers." The only solution Channing could see to this dilemma was to revert to the Indians. The language of the Indian is, he opined, "now elevated and soaring, for his image is the eagle, and now precipitous and hoarse as the cataract among whose mists he is descanting," whereas the English language seemed "enfeebled by excessive cultivation." He wished that the American Revolution had produced another Tower of Babel. In that event we might have wanted a grammar and a dictionary, but our descendants would have made a literature.[6] Noah Webster was not going to have it all his own way.

But though college graduates and political conservatives had their doubts; though Dennie in the *Port Folio* and Boston Federalists in the *Monthly Anthology* might stubbornly insist that not to follow English modes was to be totally lacking in culture, I cannot altogether agree with those scholars who attribute to the "new nationalism" after the War of 1812 the first demand for literary productions of such grandeur, power, and novelty as to constitute something unique, shaggy, and American.[7] The period from 1815 to 1850 seems rather to be the years of the Great Debate over the nature of American literature, a discussion of an issue raised before the American Revolution, continuing through the time of the French Revolution and the Napoleonic Wars, and in some sense not yet settled, since we are still arguing whether it is better to be aware of *Finnegans Wake*, W. H. Auden, and Henry James than it is to be aware of Damon Runyon, *Strange Fruit,* and the prose of Ernie Pyle. The documents of this debate include an enormous number of Phi Beta Kappa orations, addresses to literary societies, and magazine essays; they include our first books of American literary history; they include the library of anthologies poured forth in the thirties and the forties, of which those of Kettell and Griswold are most familiar; and they include such better-known titles as Bryant's "American Society as a Field for Fiction," Channing's "Remarks on National Literature," Emerson's "The American Scholar," some of Cooper's prefaces, Melville's essay on Hawthorne, Hawthorne's prefaces, and a famous passage in Longfellow's *Kavanagh.*

We ought instantly to develop an American literature—on this point everybody agreed. The question was why the proper books were so slow in coming. Why, when everything was set for a great cultural instauration, had the revolution failed? Why, as the *Portico* put it in 1818, when the American people possessed the physical, intellectual, and moral materials for future greatness, why had the hoped for "Augustan age of learning" in the United States not materialized? The Baltimore magazine looked upon *Crystalina, a Fairy Tale* "by an American," which it called undoubtedly "one of the most splendid productions of the age," read Pierpont's *Airs from Palestine* with "approbation," and said that Northmore's *Washington; or, Liberty Restored* rivaled Milton, but it still was not persuaded:

We are yet without a name distinguished in letters. But this reproach must also pass away. In forming their style and manner, let our writers emulate the ambition, diligence and zeal that have so eminently characterized our gentlemen of the sword, and the object for which they contend must be inevitably attained.[8]

In the light of the Battle of Bladensburg, this compliment to gentlemen of the sword was ambiguous in the extreme.

Why was there no certainty that the national literature was great, or bound to become so? We want, argued Henry Wheaton before the New York Athenaeum in 1824, a national language, we want patrons of literature, we want extensive libraries.[9] Our governments, state and national, Timothy Flint proclaimed in 1833, do nothing to encourage literature, we have no literary metropolis, we are dependent on Great Britain in taste, we are absorbed in politics, and we are given over to gross avarice.[10] "Meek young men," Emerson said to his Harvard audience in 1837, "grow up in libraries, believing it their duty to accept the views which Cicero, which Locke, which Bacon, have given; forgetful that Cicero, Locke, and Bacon were only young men in libraries when they wrote these books." The next year he told the literary societies of Dartmouth:

This country has not fulfilled what seemed the reasonable expectation of mankind. Men looked, when all feudal straps and bandages were snapped asunder, that nature, too long the mother of dwarfs, should reimburse itself by a brood of Titans, who should laugh and leap in the continent, and run up the mountains of the West with the errand of genius and of love. But the mark of American merit in painting, in sculpture, in poetry, in fiction, in eloquence, seems to be a certain grace without grandeur, and is itself not new, but derivative, a vase of fair outline, but empty. . . . Say, rather all literature is yet to be written.[11]

Addressing the Charlottesville Lyceum, Professor George Tucker thought a growing country had no professional niche for a merely literary man, and could see no hope for the national letters until boredom or crowding in other professions drove men of talent into writing. Then, and only then, will they, "whether it be by way of attaining a high accomplishment, of finding relief from *ennui,* or of earning a living, devote their leisure exclusively to literature." [12] The Rev. William R. Williams, at Hamilton in 1843, deplored the mechanical and utilitarian spirit of the age, the yielding to expediency and gain, false theological liberalism, and the influence of superstition upon letters; [13] and by 1845 William Gilmore Simms in the South and Joseph Rocchietti in the North were devoting acrid pamphlets to the un-American traits of American letters. Most American writers, said Simms, might as well be Europeans. Intolerance, said Rocchietti, is in the hands of the multitude, and yet in no other country does a theocracy attempt to swallow up the rights of the people to free expression.[14]

Those who argued in the affirmative were not silenced, but tended to recur to the sociological or environmental argument. At Harvard in 1821 John C. Gray appealed to the diffusion of elementary education in America, to the general spread of political intelligence, to our vast, yet unified territory, and to European envy as proof that progress in American literature was too great and manifest to be denied.[15] Charles J. Ingersoll told the American Philosophic Society in 1823 that, whatever our defects in imaginative letters, "in the literature of fact, of education, of politics, and of perhaps even science," the United States was holding its own.[16] Edward Everett insisted that "the new form of political society," a vast republican audience all reading and speaking one language, and the exciting rapidity of American growth, a perpetual stimulation to imaginative minds, must give us a great literature.[17] The native writer, said Bryant in 1825, "must show how the infinite diversities of human character are yet further varied by causes that exist in our own country," a task in which "a foreigner is manifestly incompetent."[18] At Williams College in 1835 George Bancroft insisted that the "universal diffusion of human powers" in a republic inevitably meant progress—"the great doctrine of the natural right of every human being to moral and intellectual culture"; wherefore, let the young literary aspirant "scatter the seeds of truth . . . in the deep, fertile soil of the public mind."[19] To demand an independent literary class is idle, said Verplanck at Union College in 1836, since great authors from Shakespeare to Walter Scott were "men of those mixed pursuits, that multifarious instruction" he thought also characteristic of Americans assured of a "comfortable subsistence."[20] And a variety of essayists and orators[21] argued that the United States is a Christian nation, Christianity incites the imagination to its noblest endeavors, and hence a noble literature is inevitable. In the words of the *Southern Literary Messenger* in 1845: "Literature finds the fire of its noblest inspiration glowing upon the altar of Christianity." And amid this confused and eloquent debate I find two passages too characteristic and amusing not to be quoted in full.

The first is by Dr. Samuel L. Mitchill, speaking at Schenectady in 1821 before the Alpha of New York Phi Beta Kappa and prophesying the quality of scholars yet to come:

> Hasten, O come quickly, thou season of expectation, when the proficients in benign letters and arts, doctors of philosophy, with harps and timbrels in their hands, and with crowns of bay and glory on their heads, during their stay in this world, experience a true foretaste of the next! [22]

The ambiguity of this prophecy with reference to the hereafter of scholars must strike all products of our graduate schools.

The second, singularly prophetic of that "Mom" of whom Philip Wylie complains, appears in the *Southern Literary Messenger* for 1834 and is apparently an appeal by the editor, James Heath, for a female book-of-the-month club:

> To our lovely and accomplished countrywomen, may not a successful appeal be also addressed, to lend their aid in this meritorious task. Their influence upon the happiness and destiny of society, is so extensively felt and acknowledged, that to dwell upon its various bearings and relations, would be altogether superfluous. It is to the watchful care of a mother's love, that those first principles of moral wisdom are implanted in childhood, which ripen into the blossoms and fruits of maturer years; and it is to the reproving virtues and refining tenderness of the sex, through all its mutations, from blooming sixteen to the matronly grace of forty—that man is indebted for all that is soft, and for much that is noble and wise, in his own character. It is true that there is another side to this picture. If a woman's education has itself been neglected; if she has been trained up in the paths of folly and vanity—and been taught to ornament the casket in preference to the celestial jewel it contains,—she

will neither be a fit companion for the sterner sex, nor be qualified to assume the divine responsibility of maternal instruction.
To diffuse therefore not only the benefits of moral but intellectual culture, among those whom heaven has given to restore
in part the blessings of a lost Eden—to withdraw their minds
from vain and unprofitable pursuits—to teach them to emulate
the distinguished names of their own sex, who have given lus-
tre to literature, and scattered sweets in the paths of science . . .

all this, it appears, is one of the major tasks of American
literature.[23]

Despite his reputation for mere bearishness, Cooper was
wise enough to estimate the strength and absurdity of the
Great Debate; and in *Home as Found* (1838) one notes the
mingled amusement and irony with which he listened to
the discussion. Mrs. Legend's literary party, burlesqued in
chapter six of the novel, might have occurred almost anywhere, but the dispute in chapter twenty-five between
Steadfast Dodge and Mr. Wenham, on the one hand, and
the more cosmopolitan Effingham family and its friends, on
the other, is an admirable résumé of this crucial argument,
at once heroic and absurd: "The progress of American Literature," Dodge is made to say,

is really astonishing the four quarters of the world. I believe
it is very generally admitted, now, that our pulpit and bar are
at the very summit of these two professions. Then we have
much the best poets of the age, while eleven of our novelists
surpass any of all other countries. . . . Then to what a pass
has the drama risen of late years! Genius is getting to be quite
a drug in America!

When Mr. Effingham is adjured to state what he thinks the
weakest point in American culture may be, he replies:

Provincialisms, with their train of narrow prejudices, and a disposition to set up mediocrity as perfection, under the double influence of an ignorance that unavoidably arises from a want of models, and of the irresistible tendency to mediocrity, in a nation where the common mind so imperiously rules . . . While America is so much in advance of other nations, in a freedom from prejudices of the old school, it is fast substituting a set of prejudices of its own, that are not without serious dangers.

2

However, our interest is in the development of American literary history. It is clear that certain postulates of literary history are involved in this debate. Indeed, the first three works of American literary history present the early crucial issues both of literary history and of these arguments. When in 1824–1825 John Neal contributed his papers on American writers to *Blackwood's Magazine*,[24] he argued that there were only two or three American authors who could not pass for English writers, whereas it was the allegedly British quality of American writing that discouraged the ultrapatriotic, a dichotomy that raises the whole problem of literary nationalism. Again, if Ingersoll appealed to books of fact, of education, of politics, and of science to characterize American literary production, he was but anticipating Samuel L. Knapp's *Lectures on American Literature* [25] of 1829, which include the fine arts, oratory, the lives of military and naval heroes among the literature designed "to exhibit to the rising generation something of the history of the thoughts and intellectual labours of our forefathers"; and the problem whether literary history is to be encyclopedic or selective immediately appears. And if one turns to the preface of Samuel Kettell's *Specimens of American Poetry* (1829), one finds this passage: "While the polite letters of foreign countries have been studied in such a philosophical view by the most accomplished scholars of our land, the same interesting field of observation at home has been overlooked," as if, says Kettell,

the poets of the western world could not bear some characteristic traits of their day and generation as well as the Minnesingers and Trouvères; or as if a lay of the pilgrim fathers of New England could not illustrate a point of national or individual character as effectually as the Gongorism of the Castilian rhymesters of old. This surely is a preposterous state of things,

especially since "we begin to show a national spirit in letters." [26] A moment's reflection will indicate that Kettell, like those who argue that republican institutions or Christianity or a vast landscape must profoundly affect literary development, is raising the question of the interrelation between literary art and its physical and social environment. But these are precisely the problems raised in literary histories or in discussions of literary history available to thoughtful Americans in the first part of the nineteenth century.

We date the theory of literary history from Bacon's *De Augmentis Scientiarum,* and we date its English beginnings from Warton's *History of English Poetry,* completed in 1781. But though Bacon and Warton were both known in the United States, it does not appear that the theory of the one or the method of the other had much influence. Our earlier literary historians seem rather to have turned to continental examples. And continental practice had developed two differing schools of thought, both of which were influential in the young republic.

The first of these, descending from the Renaissance, was an imitation of encyclopedic humanism and is exemplified in the work of the German Bouterwek, the Italian Tiraboschi, and the Englishman Henry Hallam. Bacon had complained that a "complete and universal History of Learning is yet wanting"; and this school set to work, as it were, to satisfy the need. We may omit Bouterwek, least influential in the United States. Tiraboschi's enormous *Storia della letteratura italiana* announces as its subject the origins and progress of the sciences in Italy and proves to be a huge encyclopedia arranged in chronological rather than alphabetical order. It begins with thirty-two sections on the literature of the Etruscans, earliest of Italians, although the learned author solemnly assures us in section twenty-six that the literature of the Etruscans has been lost, and goes its majestic way from the literature of Magna Graecia almost to Tiraboschi's own time. A glance at part three, "The Literature of Rome from its founding to the death of Augustus," reveals the encyclopedic nature of the work, for the three books and fourteen chapters discuss poetry, eloquence, grammar, rhetoric, philosophy, history, jurisprudence, mathematical writings, medicine, libraries, Greek scholars in Rome, and painting, sculpture, and architecture.

Henry Hallam's *Introduction to the Literature of Europe in the Fifteenth, Sixteenth, and Seventeenth Centuries* (1838–1839), which can still be bought from American booksellers, takes in all western Europe and is divided into chronological units, under each of which are discussed belles-lettres, classical learning, theology, philosophy, jurisprudence, mathematics, and the sciences. The chief advance of Hallam over Tiraboschi is that he is aware, even if he is but naïvely aware, of a relation between literature and society, as when he notices that the spread of cursive characters marks the greater ease of writing in the thirteenth century, or remarks of the improvement of Italian classical scholarship after 1531 that "the very extinction of all hope for civil freedom, which characterized the new period, turned the intellectual energies of an acute and ardent people towards those tranquil pursuits which their rulers would both permit and encourage." [27]

If, then, a writer like Samuel Knapp included Noah Webster's dictionary, legal statutes, the work of scientists, clergymen, and scholars, a survey of the fine arts, and the lives of military heroes in his *Lectures on American Literature,* this is not because a naïve parochialism led him to do so. Rather, he was following the best practice of European scholarship. Knapp was in good company, for a similar aim appears in work as various as Jefferson's *Notes on Virginia,* the essays of Edwin Percy Whipple, Tuckerman's books on American artists, and, in fact, so recent a compilation as the *Cambridge History of American Literature.*

Few of us, however, are satisfied with the merely encyclopedic solution of the problem of literary history, a solution which threw no light on the central question of the Great Debate. Fortunately, a second development, dating from the eighteenth century, offered a new approach to literary history. This was the tendency, beginning in the Germany of Lessing, Herder, Goethe, Schiller, and von Humboldt, to see literary development dynamically in terms of its cultural and social setting. So far as the Americans are concerned, three names from one generation and two from another were notably influential. The first group includes Madame de Staël, Simonde de Sismondi, and Friedrich Schlegel; the second group, Cousin and Villemain.

The influence of these five writers upon the American intelligence has unfortunately not yet been traced in detail, but that, in the first part of the last century, it was manifold is evident from the many critiques and articles concerning them to be found in the files of American magazines. For the sake of clarity, and conscious of doing injustice to so rich a subject, I shall, however, confine myself to one or two points only in the case of the first three of these names.

The American who read Sismondi's *Historical View of the Literature of the South of Europe* (1813) would, I think, be impressed by two ideas especially. The first is Sismondi's ardent republicanism; the second is his doctrine that isolation is necessary in the youth of a national literature if it is to become rich and independent. When Sismondi said: "I am a republican; but while preserving that ardent love of liberty transmitted me by ancestors, whose fate was united with that of two republics, and a hatred of every kind of tyranny, I hope I have never shown a want of respect for . . . time-honoured and lofty recollections," he was expressing a sentiment bound to be sympathetically received even in conservative American circles. And in view of the ardent desire of the young nation to create a literature, nothing could be more comforting than the theory of literary development set forth in chapter one of his history:

At the period when nations yet in their infancy, are animated by a creative genius, which endows them with a poetry and literature of their own, while it renders them, at the same time, capable of splendid enterprises, susceptible of lofty passions, and disposed to great sacrifices, the literature of other nations is unknown to them. Each draws from its own bosom that which best harmonizes with its nature. Eloquence, in such a nation, is the expression of natural sentiment; poetry, the play of an imagination as yet unexhausted. . . . To offer a people thus gifted with ardent genius, models which they might, perhaps, attempt to imitate, before they are capable of appreciating them, is much to be deprecated. It is better to leave them to themselves.[28]

Could anything be more flattering to American susceptibilities or more likely to induce belief that America would produce at once an original literature if only it were let alone?

The importance of literary nationalism is also stressed in the *Lectures on the History of Literature, Ancient and Modern,* by Friedrich Schlegel, a translation of which was published in Philadelphia in 1818. Under the pressure of German romantic doctrine and of resistance to Napoleon, Schlegel discussed literature as an expression of the national spirit. One reads that the two principles common to every work of imaginative worth are "the expression of those feelings which are common to all men of elevated thinking"; and "those patriotic feelings and associations peculiar to the people in whose language it is composed, and on whom it is to exert its nearest and most powerful influence." And finally:

If we look back to the history of our species, and observe what circumstances have given to any one nation the greatest advantages over others, we shall not, I think, hesitate to admit that there is nothing so necessary to the whole improvement, or rather to the whole intellectual existence of a nation, as the possession of a plentiful store of those national recollections and associations, which are lost in a great measure during the dark ages of infant society, but which it forms the great object of the poetical art to perpetuate and adorn. Such national recollections [are] the noblest inheritance which a people can possess. . . . If to these high advantages of a national poetry and national traditions, of a history abounding in subjects of meditation, of refined art, and profound science, we add the gifts of eloquence, of wit, and of a language of society adapted to all the ends of elegant intercourse, but not abused to the purposes of immorality; we have filled up the picture of a polished and intellectual people, and we have a full view of what a perfect and comprehensive literature ought to be.[29]

"National recollections and associations . . . during the dark ages of infant society" as the foundation for literary nationalism! The wide diffusion of this doctrine explains why a thousand poets struggled to turn Indian legends and colonial tales into verse; why Hawthorne complained that America was too lacking in dim and picturesque antiquity; why, even as late as 1879, Henry James wrote that American sunshine was too raw, American landscape too juvenile, and American architecture without manors, country houses, thatched cottages, cathedrals, and ivied ruins!

And finally, Madame de Staël, that "plain woman with her mouth full of ink," whom Byron so disliked—what has she to bring to the Great Debate in her two works, *The Influence of Literature upon Society*, translated and published in Boston, New York, and Philadelphia in 1813, and the famous *De l'Allemagne* of 1820? Her essential contributions to this point of view were two: she insisted that prog-

64

ress exists, that it means republican freedom, and that republican freedom means literary health; and she insisted
that Christianity, far from degrading literature and philosophy, improved and strengthened both. Dividing the
history of mankind into four eras, she made the fourth of
these the one dominated by the love of liberty, the history
of which commences with the Protestant Reformation.
She argued that literary progress is the perfecting of the
arts of thought and of expression, working necessarily
toward establishing and conserving liberty. Indeed, how
could one work upon the free will of man if one did not
have the force and truth of language to penetrate souls and
so inspire them? Writers have a Christian duty to create
the desire for new institutions in a new society; and in
studying the reciprocal relation between literature, on
the one hand, and religion, morality, and law, on the other,
she could not think of literature of the future except as
republican and Christian. "The Reformation," she said, "is
that epoch of history which has most efficaciously served
the perfectibility of the human species"—flattering doctrine for a Protestant country!—since, lacking superstition,
it gives virtue every support from rational opinion; and
though she had not visited America, she included this passage in her books:

I think it always interesting to examine what would be the
prevailing character of the literature of a great and enlightened
people, in whose country should be established liberty, political
equality, and manners in unison with its institutions: there is
but one nation in the world to whom some of these reflections
may be applied at the present day;—America. The American
literature, indeed, is not yet formed; but when their magistrates
are called upon to address themselves on any subject to the

public opinion, they are eminently gifted with the power of touching all the affections of the heart, by expressing simple truth and pure sentiments; and to do this, is already to be acquainted with the most useful secret of elegant style.[30]

The way for the reception of these theories of literary history, combining as they do sociology with moral idealism, was paved by theories of taste and criticism acceptable to American readers in the first third of the century. Professor William Charvat has found thirty-one American editions of Lord Kames's *Elements of Criticism,* nine of them published before 1835; fifty-three editions of Hugh Blair's *Lectures on Rhetoric and Belles Lettres* (1783), thirty-nine of them before 1835; and nine editions of Archibald Alison's *Essays on the Nature and Principles of Taste* (1790). The influence of these books upon magazine criticism in America was, as Charvat shows, decisive; it substantiated the theory that "literature is primarily social, and that the artist must adjust his work to the desires of established society." Moreover,

in no other period in American history has our culture been so completely and directly dominated by the professional classes; concomitantly, in no other period has the economically dominant class exhibited such an interest in the arts. This may be explained in part by the fact that the arts were not yet receiving sufficient public support to maintain native artists.[31] . . . But there were also positive factors. Materialism and the economic pressure of industrialized society had not yet divorced career and culture. The privileged classes alone could afford the necessary higher education. Moreover, they had achieved a sort of homogeneity of outlook through the rise of the Federalist party and the fear of popular outbreaks. They were, therefore, concerned with the need for control of society.[32]

Charvat's definitive study shows that during the first part of the nineteenth century American critics, principally writing for reviews and magazines, however they might differ among themselves, were acting as watchdogs of a middle-class republican Christian society. This implied no special hostility toward Europe, provided the ideas emanating from Europe could be fitted into the governing theory, and it is instructive to see how this was done. Let us take the single case of Madame de Staël, who, in the opening decades of the century, divided attention with Madame de Genlis as a leading Frenchwoman in the literary world. Magazines were interested to give American readers an impression of her personality [33] and information about her life, mostly thought of as that of a "liberal" persecuted by Napoleon.[34] The merits and defects of *Corinne* and *Delphine* were widely debated, since these novels involved both the movement of sentimentalism and the problem of the morality of fiction.[35] So, too, Constant's *Adolphe* had a considerable American press.[36] But Madame de Staël was also frequently quoted as a sociologist and political historian.[37] Reviewing Constant's *Mélanges de littérature et de politique* in 1833, the *North American Review* devoted most of its energy to summing the importance of Madame de Staël, whose

nobleness of mind, . . . grandeur of thought, and uprightness, . . . rectitude, and . . . sincere love of truth . . . distinguish her productions perhaps above those of every contemporary French author.

[In] power of considering *en masse* the character not only of one nation, but of the most opposite nations,—in taking a philosophic and general view of the state of society, and of the re-

67

mote causes of present events, she is unequalled by any writer of her own sex, in any age or country.

. . . We feel after the perusal of her pages, our mind is filled with noble ideas, with lofty sentiments, with warm affection for our kindred and our friends, with more general benevolence and good-will toward our species and with greater hopes for its amelioration. . . .[38]

In sum, the interpretation of personality and the presentation of theory were both consonant with the premises of American literary speculation. Sismondi, by reason of his republican themes, had only less appeal.[39]

If no literary history of the United States and no book of literary theory of weight and richness equal to the Europeans appeared, it was presumably because the ideas implicit or explicit in Madame de Staël, Sismondi, and Schlegel had to undergo a period of germination in their new soil. Certainly there was little in the earlier European histories of American literature to encourage emulation. *De la littérature et des hommes de lettres des Etats unis d'Amérique* by Eugène A. Vail "citoyen des Etats-unis," which appeared in Paris in 1841 is all-inclusive, gossipy, and uncritical; its intellectual level may be guessed from the first sentence of the introduction: "Literature is the perfume of a nation." What appears to be the first German history is K. Brunnemann's *Geschichte der nordamerikanischen Literatur,* of which a second edition appeared at Leipzig in 1868, but this is scarcely more than an expanded pamphlet. Of far greater merit is *Etudes sur la littérature et les moeurs des Anglo-Américains au XIX<sup>e</sup> Siècle,* by the indefatigable Philarète Chasles, published in Paris in 1851. Aside from the fact that more than half the book is devoted to British literature, another difficulty arises from the fact that Chasles spent most of his time on those writers of special interest to France, though even in this respect his management is eccentric—Franklin, Crève-coeur, and Jonathan Edwards are all discussed from pages eight through ten, whereas Gouverneur Morris occupies twenty-four pages. The unexpected amount of space given to Herman Melville (pages 118–146) is due less to an understanding of Melville than to the interest of France in Tahiti—the discussion concerns *Omoo, Typee,* and *Mardi* almost exclusively. For a similar reason, *Evangeline* has the dignity of a separate chapter. Chasles writes under the influence of De Tocqueville, whose American vogue helped to increase the institutional approach to literary history; and he has some rudimentary traces of both a sociological and a racial theory. The genius of the United States, he says, is "material and mechanic; their force lies in their good sense, their patient observation and industry. It is . . . a country without imagination because without memories." And, prophesying that the new republic is to become a mightier Europe, he concludes:

Through the phases of public or private life which we have noticed, education, politics, enterprise, position of woman, religion, passions, debates, we have always found the three [*sic*] elements of the past—Teutonic, Puritan, Anglo-Saxon, Christian—variety, liberty, tradition, labor, energy, charity. These virtues, make the force and power of present America, which lives and grows by them, not by her political institutions.

This was, of course, a social not an aesthetic judgment—one which scarcely helped the cause of literary history, though Chasles was translated and published in New York in 1852.[40] From the American point of view France was still the leading continental power; and perhaps one reason why it took so long for the ideas of Madame de Staël and her contemporary historians to germinate was French indifference to America. A student of the problem observes,

> Before 1835 American literature can hardly be said to have had a real critic in France. The straggling bibliographical notes and the incomplete accounts of such American works as appealed at all . . . seem to indicate, indeed, not any interest in American literature as such, but rather a mere mention of what was considered the least important manifestation of the intellectual life of the United States. There are certain traces of a feeling of disappointment that American literature did not immediately reflect in poetry and in oratory the idealism of liberty.[41]

The French, therefore, shortly surrendered "the right of first judgment" to the English.

But though the situation was not simple, one cannot rest satisfied with the assumption of an elder generation of scholars that the ante-bellum Great Debate over the nature of American literature was simply the expression of hostility to British condescension. So soon as we look into the arguments on the question of what American literature is and what it ought to be; so soon as we place these arguments by the side of contemporary European treatises on literary theory and literary history; so soon as we discover an American interest in these treatises, we must be struck by the identity of arguments in both classes of documents. The inference seems irresistible that not a naïve patriotism alone, but a philosophic interpretation based upon, or conscious of, European theories of the nature of literature and of its relation to society and social institutions is what these essayists and orators, these editors and reviewers were seeking to evolve. If the Great Debate produced no history of American literature more valuable than Knapp's lectures, consciously or unconsciously it laid the intellectual foundations upon which the noble structure of Moses Coit Tyler's histories was to be erected; and Tyler himself was to be influenced by European theory. Before the middle of the century the innocent arrogance of the Revolutionary epoch had transformed itself into a renewed desire to profit from European wisdom. The beginnings of American literary history rest, not in chauvinism, but in the diffusion of a theory of literary development enunciated by European writers.

## NOTES TO CHAPTER III

[1] See the famous "Letter III" of *Letters from an American Farmer* (Everyman ed.). It is notable that neither in this work nor in his *Sketches of Eighteenth Century America,* ed. Bourdin, Gabriel, and Williams (New Haven, 1925) does Crèvecoeur pay more than casual attention to the problem of academic education or the problem of literature in the New World.

[2] See *The Writings of Thomas Jefferson* (20 vols., Library ed.; Washington, 1903). For the advice to shun Europe see his letter to Bellini, dated Paris, September 30, 1785, and the more famous one to J. Bannister, Jr., Paris, October 15, 1785 (V, 151–154, 185–188); for the passage on the Americanization of the English language, see his letter to John Waldo from Monticello, August 16, 1813 (XIII, 338–347); and for his comment on the backwardness of American literature see his letter to J. Evelyn Denison from Monticello, November 9, 1825 (XVI, 129–135).

Jefferson did not join the attack on the classical languages. See his defense of Greek and Latin in a letter to John Brazier from Poplar Forest, August 24, 1819 (XV, 207–211), in which he concludes that "the classical languages are a solid basis for most, and an ornament to all the sciences."

[3] *Works in Verse and Prose, of the late Robert Treat Paine, Jun. Esq.*, ed. C. Prentiss (Boston, 1812), pp. 185, 160.

[4] Harold Milton Ellis, *Joseph Dennie and His Circle: A Study in American Literature from 1792 to 1812*, Bulletin of the University of Texas, no. 40 (July 15, 1915), "Studies in English," no. 3, p. 222. Ellis notes the inscription of Dennie's tombstone: "He devoted his life to the Literature of his Country." This is, of course, undeniable; what is in question is the conservative quality of this devotion. As Ellis remarks of the *Port Folio:* "Pretty nearly everything distinctively American came in for its share of sharp censure or mocking gibe. The typical Yankee farmer or trader, the *Jonathan* of Tyler's *Contrast*, shrewd and honest, but often unlettered and uncouth, whom, as Uncle Sam or Brother Jonathan, we have adopted as our national prototype, represented to Dennie nearly all the evils of American life which he desired to eradicate" (p. 185). He reprinted from the *New England Palladium* in 1801 a reference to Webster's projected American dictionary as a "volume of *foul* and *unclean* things," a "Noah's ark."

[5] I am indebted for much of this information to the admirable unpublished dissertation of Donald M. Goodfellow, "The Literary Life of John Quincy Adams" (Harvard, 1945). A summary appears in the *Harvard Summaries of Theses, 1943–1945* (Cambridge, Mass., 1947). See also Horace Rahskopf, "John Quincy Adams' Theory and Practice of Public Speaking," *Archives of Speech* (University of Iowa), I, 7–98 (September, 1936).

[6] See "Essay on American Language and Literature," *North American Review*, I, 307–314 (September, 1815); and "Reflections on the Literary Delinquency of America," *ibid.*, II, 33–43 (November, 1815). Even as late as 1915 the notion that the United States required its own language to develop its own literature was under debate. See the *Dial*, LVIII(686), 37–38 (January 16, 1915).

[7] Cf. chapter xx of Longfellow's *Kavanagh* where Mr. Hathaway proposes as an ideal "a national literature altogether shaggy and unshorn, that shall shake the earth, like a herd of buffaloes thundering over the praries" and Mr. Churchill responds by dryly remarking that "a man will not necessarily be a great poet because he lives near a great mountain." The general question has been surveyed by Nanette M. Ashby in "Aliment for Genius," *American Literature* VIII(4), 371–378 (January, 1937), who reaches the conclusion that "this shift in the quest for the aliments of American genius from the search for memorials of the past to an effort to find inspiration in

the power of American instruments of progress imperceptibly bridged the way from the old romanticism with its emphasis upon the past and upon the stereotyped modes of European literature to the new romanticism which glorified the present and the life about one." But this seems to me to use "romanticism" in the loosest possible sense.

An unpublished thesis by William Ellery Sedgwick, "The Problem of American Literature as Seen by Contemporary Critics, 1815–1830" (Harvard, 1934) covers fifteen years of this period more thoroughly.

[8] I have had to depend for my knowledge of the *Portico* upon the excerpts in the excellent article of J. C. McCloskey, "The Campaign of Periodicals after the War of 1812 for National American Literature," *Publications of the Modern Language Association,* L(1), 262–273 (March, 1935).

[9] Henry Wheaton, *An Address Pronounced at the Opening of the New-York Athenaeum, December 14, 1824* (New York, 1824).

[10] Timothy Flint, "Obstacles to American Literature," *Knickerbocker,* II(3), 161–170 (September, 1833).

[11] These two passages by Emerson are from "The American Scholar" and from the address entitled "Literary Ethics."

[12] Tucker's "Discourse on American Literature" was printed in the *Southern Literary Messenger,* IV(2), 80–88 (February, 1838). Despite his curious argument about boredom, Tucker thought that interstate rivalry would increase literary production and that "the West, the ardent, generous West, also shows its ambition to excel. . . . On the whole . . . the prospects . . . are no less brilliant and grand in our literature, than in our national power and opulence" (p. 88).

[13] William R. Williams, *The Conservative Principle in Our Literature* (New York, 1844).

[14] See William Gilmore Simms, *Views and Reviews in American Literature, History and Fiction, First Series* (New York, 1845), especially the first article; and Joseph Rocchietti, *Why a National Literature Cannot Flourish in the United States of North America* (New York, 1845). Simms blows hot and cold. In *Views and Reviews* he argues that the genius of the Anglo-Saxons is "too earnest, too intensely moral in its objects, for the consideration of still life except as subordinate to action" (p. 13); but in the dedication to *The Wigwam and the Cabin* (1845) he seems to think that a national literature is possible through sectionalism.

THEORY OF AMERICAN LITERATURE

[15] Gray's Phi Beta Kappa oration is in the *North American Review,* XIII(33), 478–490 (October, 1821).

[16] Ingersoll's address, "The Influence of America on the Mind" is reprinted in Joseph L. Blau's *American Philosophical Addresses, 1700–1900* (New York, 1946), pp. 17–59. He generally follows the institutional argument, and thinks that political, scientific, and "mechanical" development is most characteristic of American culture.

[17] Everett's address, "The Circumstances Favorable to the Progress of Literature in America," given before the Harvard chapter of Phi Beta Kappa is accessible in Blau, pp. 60–93.

[18] "American Society as a Field for Fiction," *North American Review,* XX (n.s. 22), 245–272 (April, 1825). The essay is a review of Miss Sedgwick's *Redwood,* and the better parts of it are in Bryant's *Prose Writings,* ed. Parke Godwin (New York, 1889), II, 351–360.

[19] "The Office of the People in Art, Government and Religion," in Blau, pp. 94–114.

[20] "The Advantages and Dangers of the American Scholar," also in Blau, pp. 115–150.

[21] See, for example, Wheaton's *Address;* H. W. Longfellow's "Defence of Poetry," *North American Review,* XXXIV, 56–78 (January, 1832); D. D. Barnard's *Address at Williams College* (1837); Job R. Tyson's *Lecture . . . before the Athenian Institute and Mercantile Library Company on the Social and Moral Influences of the American Revolution* (Philadelphia, 1838); Leonard Bacon's *Discourse before the Society of Phi Beta Kappa at Yale College, August 20, 1839,* "The Character and Functions of American Literature"; E. P. Whipple's review of Griswold's *Poets and Poetry of America* in the *North American Review,* LVIII(122), 1–39 (January, 1844); and the article by "W. C. S. of Virginia" entitled "The Present State of American Letters, the Prospect and Means of their Improvement," *Southern Literary Messenger,* XI(7), 393–400 (July, 1845) for characteristic variants.

[22] Samuel L. Mitchill, *Discourse on the State and Prospects of American Literature, delivered at Schenectady, July 24th, 1821, before the New-York Alpha of the Phi Beta Kappa Society* (Albany, 1821), p. 36.

[23] "Southern Literature," *Southern Literary Messenger,* I(1), 1–3 (August, 1834).

[24] These are conveniently reprinted in *American Writers: A Series of Papers Contributed to Blackwood's Magazine (1824–1825) by*

*John Neal,* ed. with notes and bibliography by Fred Lewis Pattee (Durham, 1937).

[25] Samuel L. Knapp, *Lectures on American Literature, with Remarks on Some Passages of American History* (New York, 1829). Knapp had briefly discussed the problem of American poetry and the interrelation between literary genius and natural scenery in his *Letters of Shahcoolen, A Hindu Philosopher, Residing in Philadelphia; to His Friend El Hassan, an Inhabitant of Delhi* (Boston, 1802). The sixth letter is a sympathetic review of the productions of the Connecticut Wits; and in the seventh, after an enthusiastic series of paragraphs on the American landscape, we learn that *"Here* nature seems to have gloried in her might, and to have put forth the highest efforts of creative energy. Such scenes are calculated to seize the imagination, and hurry it into poetical enthusiasm. This effect I have frequently witnessed, as produced upon American minds. Their poets frequently celebrate their rivers, mountains, cataracts and plains. . . . Indeed there is no deficiency of poetical talents in the nation at large, and the whole natural scenery of the country, tends to fill the mind with grand and sublime conceptions, and in no small degree with sensations of beauty" (pp. 87–88).

[26] Samuel Kettell, *Specimens of American Poetry, with Critical and Biographical Notices* (3 vols.; Boston, 1829), I, iv, v.

[27] Henry Hallam, *Introduction to the Literature of Europe in the Fifteenth, Sixteenth, and Seventeenth Centuries* (4 vols. in 2; New York, 1880), I, 75, 326.

[28] J. C. L. Simonde de Sismondi, *Historical View of the Literature of the South of Europe,* translated by Thomas Roscoe (2 vols.; New York, 1827), I, 9–10; 25–26. The passage "I am a republican" is quoted in the Bohn Library edition of this same work (2 vols.; 3d ed.; London, 1850), I, 9.

[29] *Lectures on the History of Literature, Ancient and Modern. From the German of Frederick Schlegel* (2 vols.; Philadelphia, 1818), I, 6–7, 14–15, 19.

[30] *The Influence of Literature upon Society. Translated from the French of Madame de Stael Holstein* (2 vols.; Boston, 1813), *passim.*

[31] In an interesting dissertation (unpublished) at Harvard, "The Dissatisfaction with the Conditions facing the Literary Artist in the United States from 1830 to the Civil War" (1948), G. Ferris Cronkhite has studied a functional relationship between individual theories of genius held by writers and the ability of the writer to support himself.

[32] William Charvat, *The Origins of American Critical Thought, 1810–1835* (Philadelphia, 1936), p. 5. The information about editions of the Scottish writers on taste may be found on pp. 30–31.

[33] A description of a visit to Madame de Staël extracted from *Letters from Geneva and France* appears in the *Port Folio* for August 20, 1808, and a biographical estimate in the same magazine in August, 1816. Another sketch may be found in the *Analectic Magazine* for September, 1817; and the same magazine in March, 1819, reprinted a letter from *Blackwood's Edinburgh Magazine* commenting on the lady's "generous, superior soul, and sense of dignity." A long analysis, based on De Saussure's life and apparently reprinted from an English periodical, appears in the *National Recorder* for August 26, 1820, where the reader learns that "her soul had more life in it than that of ordinary persons," but that her life "teaches us that the gifts of sensibility and the imagination are dangerous to our fallen state." The *North American Review* for July, 1820, spoke of her as "a most extraordinary woman, and the greatest female that has ever written," and the article was reprinted in the *Literary and Scientific Repository* for June, 1820. These are a few examples among many.

[34] In addition to curiosity about the life of Madame de Staël there was apparently a considerable interest in her literary earnings. The *Analectic Magazine*, in August, 1817, noted that her memoirs of her father was sold for £4,000 to an association of English, French, and German publishers (booksellers) and would appear simultaneously in three languages, and this information was widely reprinted. See, for example, the *American Monthly Magazine and Critical Review* for June, 1817 (p. 128). A variant appears in the *North American Review* for May, 1817, where the sum is 100,000 francs for her *Views of the Principal Occurrences of the French Revolution*.

For biographical sketches, see *Port Folio*, August, 1816; *Analectic Magazine*, September, 1817; *American Monthly Magazine and Critical Review*, December, 1817; *North American Review*, July, 1820; *American Monthly Review*, September, 1832. Her death and funeral received immediate notice; see, for example, *Boston Weekly Messenger*, September 11, 1817; *Analectic Magazine*, January, 1818.

[35] Representative comment may be found in the *North American Review* for July, 1820, the article being by T. Parsons. Of *Delphine* he wrote: "Its popularity was very great when it first appeared, but has since died away. Once read largely and every where, it now descends from the shelf of a circulating library scarcely once in a

twelve month. It is certainly written in a most captivating style, and with a brilliancy and energy of language, that all French literature can scarcely equal; but as a story it is very dull, and its morality is— or rather is not—very questionable." And of *Corinne* he remarked that it is the novel by which she is best known. "Faulty, very faulty, as it certainly is, in the grotesque mixture of the philosopher, the antiquarian and the novelist, it must be regarded with admiration for its splendid literary execution and its strains of touching, powerful eloquence. Of the story we need say nothing, as it must be familiar to our readers" (pp. 134, 137).

[36] See the *Analectic Magazine*, September, 1817; *American Monthly Magazine and Critical Review*, October, 1817; the article reviewing Chenier's *Tableau historique* in the *American Quarterly Review*, June, 1827. Most of the notices of Constant have something to say about Madame de Staël.

[37] See, for notices or quotations, *American Review of History and Politics*, October, 1811; *General Repository and Review*, January, 1812; *Analectic Magazine*, June, 1813; *ibid.*, December, 1813; *ibid.*, June, 1814; *ibid.*, March, 1818; *ibid.*, July, 1818; *ibid.*, August, 1818; *National Recorder*, August 26, 1820; *North American Review*, July, 1820; *ibid.*, January, 1822.

[38] The *North American Review*, XXXVII(80), 1–20 (July, 1833). The article is by the future Madame Calderon de la Barca.

[39] The author of *The History of the Italian Republics of the Middle Age* seemed to the *American Register or Summary Review* (I, 335–337; 1817) "the first historian of his time," his work displaying "the highest order of excellence, both in form and substance." (This follows the *Edinburgh Review*.) The same article found the *Literature of the South of Europe* a "must" volume, and classed it with De Staël and Schlegel. The *American Quarterly Review*, December, 1832, eulogized him; and the *Analectic Magazine* in 1818–1819 printed extracts from the *Literature of the South of Europe*, as had the *American Register and Summary Review* in 1817.

[40] I have quoted from the translation, *Anglo-American Literature and Manners* (New York, 1852), pp. 6, 306, a botched job of translation and condensation. The Harvard College Library copy formerly belonged to Herman Melville. The book is obviously designed for propaganda; thus, a long discussion of Audubon (pp. 57–94) is used as a stick to beat the French with for neglecting their colonies. On the other hand, Chasles was a person of penetration. For example, he said that the "mighty talent" of Cooper displayed defects originating

77

in the "doctrinal severity and Calvinist rigidity inherent in the Anglo-American colonies," and though Cooper was not a Puritan, this is a valuable *aperçu*.

41 Harold Elmer Mantz, *French Criticism of American Literature before 1850* (New York, 1917), p. 155.

# IV

# "The Arms of the Anglo-Saxons"

AMERICAN interest in the literary theories of Madame de Staël, Sismondi, and Friedrich Schlegel helped to shape a vague theory of American literature, particularly of literature in relation to American institutions, during the first half of the nineteenth century.[1] That theory was usually warmly republican and sometimes violently anti-British,[2] but there was a philosophic connection between these two attitudes, since, if you assumed that republican institutions must call into being a virtuous literature, you necessarily repudiated the monarchical institutions, including literature, of the British Isles. Yet whereas most writers before 1850 denounced or envied British literature as the chief obstacle to native genius; and despite the hostility between the British upper class and the North during the Civil War—a hostility which, added to previous controversies, might reasonably be expected to increase American distrust of British criticism—almost every history of American literature from the sixties to 1913, when John Macy published his *Spirit of American Literature* and inaugurated the modern interpretation of the subject, not only insisted upon measuring American writers by British standards, but also claimed that American literature was a branch of English letters, a subordinate, if locally interesting, expression of the Anglo-Saxon spirit. Why and how did this amazing revolution come about?

Even before the Civil War there were, of course, conservatives who advised the Americans to be content with that inferior station to which it had pleased God to call them in the cultural hegemony of Great Britain.[3] But beginning about the middle of the century, strengthening in the sixties,[4] and burgeoning in the last third of the century, three several forces strengthened the Anglophile tradition. One was a new development of historical interest; the second was the spread of New England culture; and the third was the growth of English departments in American schools and colleges.

The Civil War strengthened American nationalism and widened the public for historical writing. During and after the struggle there appeared a library of books by prisoners of war narrating their sufferings; of autobiographies by private soldiers and minor officers; and, later, of company and regimental histories, all finding new readers for historical material. In the seventies and eighties volumes by statesmen and generals, based on official records, were pouring forth; and in the eighties the climax came with the serial publication of the famous *Battles and Leaders of the Civil War* and of the Nicolay-Hay *Abraham Lincoln: A History.*[5] American history again became dramatic.

Moreover, a generation of historians was touched by a struggle which they knew to be crucial. Among those who served in the northern armies were Charles Francis Adams, James Schouler, and E. B. Andrews. In the case of Schouler we see the immediate effects of the conflict, for battle left him deaf, this affliction led him into historical writing, and his *United States under the Constitution, 1783–1865,* which began publication in 1880, had for its focus and climax the issues and the tragedy of the struggle. Even when the historian was too young to 'list for a soldier, as was James Ford Rhodes, the war affected him. In the sixties Rhodes was a high-school student in Cleveland, where the principal assured the boys that they were living in the midst of events as historic as those in the life of Greece and Rome, a speech to which the author of the great *History of the United States from the Compromise of 1850* traced the interest that led him to abandon finance for writing.

This renewed historical activity was fed from other springs. In the United States the period is marked by the creation or enlargement of historical societies, historical libraries, and professional associations; by the introduction of courses in American history in schools and colleges and its recognition as a subject for graduate study; and by an increase in the writing of monographs and technical works for the trained historian and of textbooks for both elementary and advanced instruction. And this activity [6] implied a shift in method and emphasis, a shift briefly described in the influential Channing-Hart *Guide to the Study of American History,* which, appearing in 1896, summed up the development thus:

> It is only within the last few years that American history has been regarded by educators either as a liberal study or as a serious subject deserving scientific treatment. This is due to the fact that the earlier books on this theme were designed to commemorate the supposed deeds of some ancestor, or to arouse the

patriotism of American youth by the relation of stories of doubtful historical foundation and of very questionable value from an ethical point of view.

The editors rejoiced that "the seed of scientific treatment of history has begun to germinate" and that the habit of reading history is "everywhere encountered." [7]

However, the scientific treatment of American history proved in certain hands a curiously romantic affair. The method was European, a method especially, though not solely, associated with German historical research; and the influence of the German school [8] upon American historical writing in the seventies and eighties was immense. Justin Winsor, whose editing of the *Narrative and Critical History of America* (1889) was a triumph for the new method, studied at Heidelberg. Andrew Dickson White went to Berlin; Charles Kendall Adams lived in Germany, France, and Italy; J. W. Burgess went to Göttingen, Leipzig, and Berlin; E. B. Andrews studied in Germany; Herbert Baxter Adams took his Ph.D. at Heidelberg; and Albert Bushnell Hart took his at Freiburg. And when these young men came back, filled with enthusiasm for the new learning, with its thoroughness, its textual exactitude, its trust in comparative politics and its racial overtones, they established their research seminars at Michigan, at Cornell, at Columbia, at Johns Hopkins, at other universities; and set their students, in place of reading the elegant masters of the past, the task of solving a problem which would in turn lead to a monograph so substantial that no subsequent historian could overthrow it.

Enthusiasm for German methodology brought with it an enthusiasm for the work of contemporary English historians working in the same racial spirit. The writings of

Stubbs, Green, Gardiner, Freeman, and others had particular vogue; [9] and the visit of E. A. Freeman to the United States had a profound effect. In 1881–1882 he delivered at the Lowell Institute in Boston and at the Peabody Institute in Baltimore the lectures known as "The English People in Its Three Homes"; and at Cornell, Yale, and Pennsylvania, another set entitled "The Practical Bearings of General European History." The first series demonstrated that there were three Germanys—Germany, England, the United States; the practical bearings of history in the second took this form:

> To you, citizens of this newer England, transplanted children of the elder England, common children with us of the oldest England of all, I would, before all things, preach this lesson. When you read the history of Aryan Europe, you are reading the records of a kindred folk, in which you have the interest of kinsmen. . . . As of old wherever Hellênes dwelled, there was Hellas, so we should deem that, wherever the English folk dwell, there is England.[10]

At Johns Hopkins, Freeman's informal lectures were devoted to the historical geography of southeastern Europe, the "Eastern Question," and kindred themes,[11] but the racial spirit was not forgotten; under the editorship of Herbert Baxter Adams, the first of the "Johns Hopkins University Studies in Historical and Political Science" (1882) carried as its epigraph Freeman's famous apothegm: "History is past Politics and Politics present History," and opened with an admiring essay by the editor on "Mr. Freeman's Visit to Baltimore." The substance of the monograph, *An Introduction to American Institutional History,* was, *mirabile dictu,* by Freeman himself; and he not only argued that the institutions of New England and Virginia took their place "in the general course of English and of Teutonic history" but included the remarkable theory that Louisiana, Missouri, and Wisconsin were the "Romance lands of America" and had "adopted the traditions of their Teutonic neighbours by the . . . effectual process of receiving their Teutonic neighbours within their borders." [12] The second monograph in the series obediently dealt with *The Germanic Origin of New England Towns,* and was by the devoted Adams.

In the name of scientific history, then, evolution educed the New England town meeting indifferently from the English parish and the Teutonoburg forest; and so seductive did racial Darwinism prove that even Henry Adams wrote: "I flung myself into the arms of the Anglo-Saxons in history." By and by Teddy Roosevelt was to attribute the winning of the West principally to the strenuous virtues of Teutonic males. Adherents taught the political and cultural unity of the Teutonic races; John Fiske lectured up and down the land on the virility of Anglo-Saxon federalism; and in his *Transit of Civilization* (1900) Edward Eggleston found it necessary, he said, to go to England to explain the characteristics of the American seventeenth century. We can sum up the movement by recurring to the Channing-Hart *Guide,* which, in spite of Channing's opposition to Anglo-Saxon racism, threw out pre-Columbian America as not worth studying and dismissed all Latin America "because the life of the natives there except in Peru possesses little interest; and because the Latin-Americans have made no significant contribution to the world's stock of social and political experience." It is not boastful, they soberly wrote, "to say that American history is principally the story of the development of the United

States of America, from the earliest English settlements; for the chief service America has rendered the human race in the development of the great federal republic." [13]

## 2

Triumph in the Civil War was, from the Northern point of view, the triumph of righteousness—of that New England righteousness which had prophesied the Federal Union in the Mayflower Compact and which, in the providence of God, stretched its cultural empire from Maine to the Pacific Coast. The westward expansion of New England was a kind of Protestant crusade,[14] the spirit of which is well expressed in resolutions adopted at Castleton, Vermont, in 1836, by a colony about to settle Vermontville, Michigan:

> Whereas, the enjoyment of the ordinances and institutions of the Gospel is in a great measure unknown in many parts of the western country; and whereas, we believe that a pious and devoted emigration is to be one of the most efficient means, in the hands of God, in removing the moral darkness which hangs over a great portion of the valley of the Mississippi . . . We agree, when we have arrived in the western country, . . . to form ourselves into such a community as will enable us to enjoy the same social and religious privileges which we leave behind.[15]

The moral sentiment here is more admirable than the geography, but such was the evangelical spirit which, in the shape of the Yale band, the Iowa band, or of a whole community, evangelized the West against atheism, infidelity, the slaveholder, and the pope. And everywhere the westering flood—so thick that in 1821 the Rev. Timothy

Dwight thought New York state might become a New England colony [16]—left as a rich alluvial deposit New England names, New England architecture, New England churches, and, above all, New England teachers and New England literary light.

Thus the public school system of Michigan was largely shaped by the Rev. John D. Pierce of New Hampshire; and when Iowa created its schools, it called in Horace Mann and Amos Dean of Massachusetts and Vermont. "New England" colleges like Marietta, Muskingum, Oberlin, Olivet, Grinnell, Carleton, Beloit, Knox, Washburn, Mills, Pomona, and Whitman dominated cultural values; and universities as various as Western Reserve, Michigan, Kansas, and California were begun and shaped by New England minds. And always the intellectual focuses of this vast, invisible empire were Boston and Concord, Harvard and Yale, the Andover Theological Seminary and Dartmouth College, the publishing house of Ticknor and Fields and the editorial office of the *Atlantic Monthly* or the *North American Review*. You read in the essays of William Dean Howells about the pride of Columbus, Ohio, in the town's two contributors to the *Atlantic;* [17] and in the pilgrimages of Howells, Garland, and Bret Harte to Boston and Cambridge, the removal of Mark Twain and Charles Dudley Warner to Hartford, Connecticut, you see the working of the spell. Moreover, and most important for us, the standardization of American authors—the creation of the canon of Great Names in our literature—is the product of this New England empire, more specifically of Ticknor and Fields and their publishing successors. Outside of Boston-born Franklin, of Bryant, Emerson, Thoreau, Longfellow, Lowell, Holmes, and Mrs. Stowe, there might be some salvation for Irving and Cooper, a little less for Poe, but almost none for Melville, Whitman, and Twain.[18] You read in Richardson's influential *American Literature* (1886–1888) that Melville was a popularity seeker, and in Barrett Wendell's *Literary History of America* (1900) that Melville wrote some books about the South Seas [19]—but that is all. He did not fit into the pattern of moral idealism central to that New England culture which was the last, best flowering of the Anglo-Saxon race. Said Barrett Wendell: "[We are disposed] with good old English commonsense, to follow those lines of conduct which practice has proved safe and which prudence has pronounced admirable." [20] American literature was not merely part of the general Aryan tradition, its greatness lay in expressing New England idealism, Protestant and moral in tone. Wrote Richardson:

> The critic of American literature should be thoroughly acquainted with both English and American political, social, and literary history; should perceive clearly that in England and America is a dominant and assimilating Saxon folk, working out a similar problem on similar lines.[21]

A primer of American literature which Richardson put together in 1878, aided by one H. A. Clark, largely for use in the schools, sold 70,000 copies and was but one of many similar books [22] by various authors.

### 3

Given this enthusiasm for American history, given the expansion of New England culture, given the supposition that American letters were almost a New England monopoly, it might reasonably be inferred that the higher study of the national letters would develop step by step with the higher study of the national history. It did not so develop; and if we ask why, when the study of American history went forward, the study of American literature went backward, we must recur to our curious enthusiasm for German methods, this time in philology. The universities did not create chairs in American literature as they had in American history; they created departments of English instead.

Although the proliferation of departments of English has been of the profoundest importance for the culture of the country, the history of their development is almost an untouched field. As early as 1798 Jefferson had urged the value of Anglo-Saxon as a study; and by 1825 George Blaetterman at the University of Virginia was giving some instruction, however vague, in that tongue. He was succeeded in 1840 by Charles Kraitsir, who yielded place in 1844 to the immensely influential Maximilian Schele de Vere, a Swede by race, a Prussian by birth, a German Ph.D., the inaugurator of systematic instruction in comparative philology of the Germanic languages, and one of the most widely influential teachers the country has ever known. Anglo-Saxon is said to have been taught at Randolph-Macon College as early as 1839. In 1841–1845 W. C. Fowler lectured on Anglo-Saxon at Amherst where, as Francis A. March remembered, Anglo-Saxon books were so rare that Fowler held them up before the class as a natural scientist displays rare minerals or precious stones. In 1848 John R. Thompson, pleading for the school of letters at Charlottesville, printed in the *Southern Literary Messenger* (September) an influential essay, giving a historical sketch of the languages of Europe, with special attention to the rise and progress of English; and in that same year Louis F. Klipstein, a South Carolinian of German extraction, published the first Anglo-Saxon grammar to be issued in the United States. This was reissued in 1849 with an introduction by Orville Horwitz of Baltimore, together with two volumes of *Analecta Anglo-Saxonica* edited by Klipstein. But Fowler complained that there were not three men in the whole country who understood the language, and Kraitsir in 1852 lamented the general neglect of linguistic study.[23]

Indeed, if we put aside the famous *Lectures on the English Language* by George P. Marsh at Columbia in 1858–1859, we may say that the introduction of Germanic philology and the creation of English departments in our colleges and universities followed the Civil War. In the South, English was mainly neglected, despite these pioneers, until the end of the conflict; and as late as 1878 Noah Porter of Yale was hopefully declaring that colleges which had substituted English for the classics had not been sustained by public opinion.[24] But Porter was wrong. Germanic philology overran academic institutions like a disease, and even threatened the high schools. Men like Schele de Vere at Virginia, Price at Columbia, Harrison at Washington and Lee, Fortier at Tulane, Corson at Cornell, Bright at Johns Hopkins, Whitney at Yale, and Child at Harvard—a whole generation of enthusiastic philologists routed the classics and created Ph.D.'s in their own images. Bright alone is said to have fathered fifty-nine. By 1875 the United States Commissioner of Education found twenty-three colleges teaching Anglo-Saxon. Looking back on this report in 1892 at a meeting of the Modern Language Association, Francis A. March noted that eighteen intervening years had seen a prodigious advance:

> This Anglo-Saxon study, delightful and important in itself to specialists, seems also to be necessary for a solid and learned support of Modern English in college. The early professors had no recondite learning applicable to English, and did not know what to do with classes in it. They can now make English as hard as Greek.[25]

The oddity of this argument was overlooked in the general enthusiasm. At Harvard, Child is said to have kept photographs of Wilhelm and Jacob Grimm on his study wall, and the fact is symbolical, for the intent was to reproduce in the New World the cloistral dedication to pure linguistic knowledge of the Old.

The aim of the new crusade was racial, historical, and moral. "There can be," said Professor Garnett in 1876, "no historical study of English without a knowledge of its oldest forms, that is, of the Anglo-Saxon language itself." [26] The Bible, according to G. Stanley Hall and Max Müller, was "the last word of Aryan man." [27] "If there is one thing more than another," wrote Professor Sears of the University of Vermont in 1886,

> about which the American of the present day is concerned, it is his ancestry. He would rather know who was his grandfather in the year 1600, than to know who will be the next president. To find out who this ancestor was he will cross the Atlantic to England, search town records, look for the flag-stone under which he was laid in the parish church, and find . . . memorial brasses on the walls.

These ancestors—at least the Anglo-Saxon part of them—were

men of noble disposition, destined to produce a better people out of the ruins of the later Roman world. Master of himself, each man of them had his own home on his own land; and if the commonwealth received aught from him, it was because he chose to give it.

. . . This century, with all its luxury, is showing . . . some of that temper which belonged to the old days of Hrolf Ganger, and of Hengist and Horsa. It is not exactly a piratical age, because piracy has gone out of fashion: but there is the same spirit of adventure into new regions and new lands. . . .

Old English, furthermore, was good for advertising, where space is valuable—its words are shorter.[28] Some flatly denied that the Anglo-Saxons were a disorderly folk; [29] others argued that elementary Old English would lead the young to "philosophize a little on the relation of the language used in a description of an event to the actual detail of the event itself"; [30] one held with Jefferson that "if we study Homer to learn the early poetic working of the Hellenic mind, the beginnings of ancient culture, we should study Old English poetry to learn the early manifestation of the Teutonic mind, the beginnings of modern culture"; [31] and men heatedly argued, apparently on the theory that ontogeny should repeat phylogeny, that elementary Anglo-Saxon should be introduced into the high schools—it was no more difficult than Latin. Moreover,

along with its simplicity of style let the boy and girl learn something of the rugged strength of his fathers. . . . Yes, let every English American youth thank God that he is descended from that plucky race that under Danish invasion, and Norman conquest and contempt, clung with unyielding tenacity to the native speech, and bequeathed it to him, his richest inheritance in the nineteenth century.[32]

English professors increased. Of course, the specialists were never satisfied—in 1884 T. W. Hunt of Princeton declared that "in the great body of our colleges . . . the place of English is quite subordinate to that of all other related departments" [33]—but when in 1894 *The Dial* surveyed some twenty representative colleges and universities, it was evident that the new department had come to stay.[34] The period saw the creation of learned monographs in stately series and of philological journals supposed to rival science in the flawless impersonality of their contents—the "Harvard Studies and Notes in Philology" (1882), *Modern Language Notes* (1886), the *Journal of English and Germanic Philology* (1897), the "Yale Studies in English" (1898), and many more. The training of even high-school teachers, one enthusiast argued, should be philological; [35] and another, with the same end in view, wanted to rise from "a somewhat formal examination of phraseology and structure to a real philological study of the tongue in its content and its great linguistic changes, its inner spirit, and its possibilities," a method that would, he argued, bring "discipline" [36] into English teaching. Even the popular magazines argued the cause; [37] and if, in the eighties, the *Academy* had to crusade for English, by the nineties every educational journal was insisting that English instruction was primary, essential, and central. Indeed, as late as 1910 a standard book on the training of English teachers had seriously to examine and refute the notion that high-school students should be required to learn something about the Indo-Aryan stock, Germanic languages, the characteristics of Old, Middle, and Modern English, and "such information regarding historical English, grammar, phonetics, etymology, and cognate matter as may be suited to his comprehension." [38]

To the specialist in linguistic studies "philology" was of course a broad and noble discipline, which included everything from phonemes to comparative literature,[39] but in fact the English department developed a split personality. As Payne put it, "The English scholars in our universities are, almost without exception, either literary critics or masters of linguistic science; they are rarely, if ever, both at once." [40] Teachers of literature found themselves in competition with linguists for respectability and place, and the resulting rivalry took on opposite and amusing characteristics. On the one hand, the all-pervading Germanic spirit in scholarship required them to stress the importance of literary works remote in time and significance from ordinary Americans; on the other hand, a continuing stream of propaganda fed the fire of enthusiasm. Were not Gray, Goldsmith, Shakespeare, Chaucer, *Beowulf,* American possessions? Did we lose our cultural heritage by crossing the Atlantic? Wrote Albert Stanburrough Cook:

The pride and interest of Americans in England's literature; . . . the craving for culture in a form which promises so much return for so little expenditure of effort; the admiration for our speech, because it is our own, because of its wide diffusion and sway, and because of the great works by which it has been illustrated; and the need and desire to employ the language as a means of communication, of persuasion, and of artistic achievement—these, seconded by the whole democratic and scientific trend of the century, by the interest of other races in their own vernaculars, and by the necessity of unifying our heterogeneous population on the basis of a common speech and common sentiments, have not only multiplied magazines and newspapers, and cheapened books, but have introduced courses in English into schools and colleges of every grade, and taxed the energies and resources of every teacher of the subject. Beginning sporadically . . . the movement . . . has tended to absorb the currents of individual opinion, and to render them all unconsciously tributary to a distant and perhaps as yet dimly perceived end.[41]

"We insist," said Hunt, "that every American College should be instinct with English literary thought and life,"[42] and as a result of this sweeping success American sophomores, who had never seen a nightingale, and had not the slightest comprehension of the meaning of "the boast of heraldry," obediently traced the stream of "English literature" to its remotest wellsprings.

I have omitted from the paragraph by Cook an unimportant phrase, for what he wrote was "The pride and interest of Americans in England's literature and that of our own country." But Cook had no real interest in American literature, which found few defenders and no crusaders. It was in vain for Lounsbury, amid his other chores, to publish good books on Cooper and Charles Dudley Warner; it was in vain, at an early meeting of the Modern Language Association (founded in 1883) for Albert H. Smyth to argue for American literary studies; it was in vain for Underwood to affirm that "our own literature must be considered as the best part of our history, and the just basis of our national pride."[43] Smyth was only a high-school teacher, Underwood was merely interested in national education; and from the majestic distance of *Beowulf* and that high Asian plateau whence sprang the Aryan tongues, American literature was "contemporary," a mere upstart, a parvenu no better than Stevenson. Scholarly dignity sometimes descended as low as Charles II, and daring persons like Corson at Cornell might teach a course in Browning, but respectability preferred the anfractuosities of the *Harrowing of Hell,* observations on fourteenth-century English, and comparing grammatical forms in Old English, Sanskrit, Gothic, Old Saxon, Old Frisian, Old Norse, and Old High Germanic. An occasional professor gave a third of his time to the national literature, but not until the nineties did college courses in the American field increase at all, and even these were elementary. Moreover, these centered principally upon that part of the American scene likest the Old World, the New England writers continuing to be the most respectable part of the teaching of American literature, whether at the college level or that of the secondary school.[44]

The effect of philological righteousness upon the higher study of the national letters was of course disastrous. As late as 1939 an editorial in the *North American Review* remarked that "our academic condescension toward our own culture has always amazed the more intelligent foreign visitors," and lamented the lack of a good history of American literature, of American architecture, of American painting, and even of American political development.[45] About ten years earlier Ferner Nuhn, in an article entitled "Teaching American Literature in American Colleges," began by quoting Whitman: "America herself? I sometimes question whether she has a corner in her own house"; and, though he listed a rising generation of scholars, and discovered an increase in doctoral dissertations, found that one general survey course for undergraduates was considered adequate in most colleges; observed that, measured in course terms, American literature was about as un-

95

important as Scandinavian, that ignorance of the field was no bar to writing a dissertation in it, and that no more than half a dozen institutions offered even a modicum of instruction in the field. Even where instruction was offered, he found that the tendency was not to inquire into what American literature contributes to American culture, but to ask what it contributes to English literature. His own suggestion was the organization of a department of American literature in order to create "something like a decent academic respect for the natural culture of the Republic." [46] The suggestion has not been adopted.

Meanwhile a concomitant revolution took place in the public schools. The private academies, faithful to the injunction of the British Educational Report of 1864, clung to Latin and Greek; but the schools for *hoi polloi* before the Civil War were, as we have seen, supplied with readers by Webster, Pierpont, Bingham, Town, McGuffey, and others, the spirit of which was often chauvinistic.[47] Moreover, the contents of these readers were often intended for oral recitation—for Friday afternoon "speaking," for declamation, for oratory—and were therefore a sympathetic medium for presenting selections from public writing, orations, and those serious discussions of political and general themes which constitute a prominent element in earlier American literary production.[48] But after 1875 this situation altered. Not to "speak well" but to be "well read" became the dominant cultural aim, and in the light of this more sophisticated ideal, the old patriotic glow began to dim its ineffectual fires. A report on English in the secondary schools of Massachusetts, printed in 1888, found small use for "English and American patriotic eloquence," but reported with pride on the "abundant evidence" of "a very encouraging awakening to a higher appreciation of the educational value of English literature." [49] Two years earlier, a New England commission of colleges, in response to an appeal from the New England Association of Colleges and Preparatory Schools, agreed on a uniform list of books from which subjects for English essays as entrance requirements should be chosen; and in 1893 the Association of Colleges and Preparatory Schools of the Middle States and Maryland set up a parallel list. The formula goes back to a Yale requirement of 1892 stipulating that entering students should have a knowledge of certain English classics. Thus the famous list of College Entrance Requirements was fastened upon the country. It was what English departments wanted, and it was what they got; and if American authors lingered among these requirements, they were reduced to the position of a minor dependency, amusingly illustrated in 1903 by Fred Newton Scott's discussion of how to train English teachers. They must, so runs his text, "be well read in English literature and English literary history," and a footnote explains: "The word 'English' will be used here and hereafter in the sense of English and American." But when we return to the text, we find his illustrative material is drawn from *Silas Marner, Ivanhoe, The Vicar of Wakefield,* the de Coverley papers, Macaulay, Carlyle, Burke, *The Rime of the Ancient Mariner, The Princess,* Milton's minor poems, *Comus, Macbeth*—and *The Last of the Mohicans!* The proportion of twelve to one is about the proportion of interest in the higher study of American literature during the height of the philological excitement.[50] It became a mere footnote to English departments; and it was sometimes neglected even in the high schools.

4

In the high schools, moreover, a New England version of American literature was taught as a branch of British culture; and for its teaching scores of elementary histories and anthologies were produced, so much alike as to awaken, in the words of Fred Lewis Pattee, the feeling, if not of conspiracy, at least of collusion. They all assumed (in the language of one of them) that American letters are but "the continuation of English literature within the limits of what has become the United States, by people English in their speech, English to a considerable extent by inheritence, and English in the original character of their civilization." [51] Two years after the publication of this book, the foreign-born population of the country was more than 15,500,000; almost 1,300,000 Americans could not speak English, an increase of more than 50 per cent per 100,000 of the population in half a century, and the United States was already embarked upon that policy of cultural pluralism which marks American eclecticism in the arts. But the literary histories stuck to the party line. They all conscientiously announced that they were going to trace the effect of a new environment upon this branch of the "Anglo-Saxons," and they all failed to do so, for they were obsessed by an idea that "our true place in literary history is as one of the literatures of . . . greater England." [52] They all conscientiously explained that we were a young people without defining either "people" or "youth"; they all equated Americanism in literature with "idealism," "democracy," "a thorough-going optimism," "healthy joy in life," or other vague, meliorative phrases, and most of them

98

deplored the fact that Americans make money. Said Mary Fisher in her *General Survey of American Literature* (1899), which, we are assured, grew out of classroom experience, the history of American genius is a record of "material prosperity." "It is, for the most part, the history of prosperous docters, lawyers, college professors, editors, and public officials, to whom literature was not the first supreme aim, but an elegant accomplishment that waited on bread-winning." [53] The inconsistency that the British, a nation of shopkeepers, produced the very literature which held the good lady in awe, troubled neither Miss Fisher nor any of her contemporaries. It was useless for John Nichol, in the best treatise on American literature published in Great Britain during the century, to remark that freshness and comprehensiveness seemed to him, after twenty years of study, the most conspicuous advantages of belles-lettres in the United States.[54] The handbooks were determined to reunite the severed portions of the Anglo-Saxon world.

Out of this flood of racism, Anglophilism, and jejune theorizing three scholars emerged who, sharing the New England predilections and the racial prejudices of their period, nevertheless laid the foundation for the modern study of American letters. They were Moses Coit Tyler, whose two great works, *A History of American Literature, 1607–1765* (1878) and *The Literary History of the American Revolution* (1897), each in two volumes, may here, despite differences in method, count as a single whole; Charles F. Richardson, author of *American Literature, 1607–1885* (1886–1888), also in two volumes, which contains a mature statement of the problem of literary history but which unfortunately does not carry through its own program; and Barrett Wendell, the bias of whose *Literary History of America* (1900) is evident in Professor Pattee's proposal to retitle it *A Literary History of Harvard University, with Incidental Glimpses of the Minor Writers of America*. All three were university professors—Tyler at Michigan and Cornell, Richardson at Dartmouth, and Wendell in Cambridge; and all three were touched with the historical zeal I earlier sketched, Tyler being one of the founders of the American Historical Association.

If we consider these books in reverse order, we note that Anglophilism is thickest in Barrett Wendell, who shuttles back and forth between Great Britain and Boston in a succession of introductory chapters which virtually ignore all the rest of Europe. Inasmuch as Wendell made a special study of the British seventeenth century, much that he says of that age still has value, despite the fact that seventeenth-century studies have shifted ground since he wrote, and despite his curious assumption that in seventeenth-century New England "heart-burnings and doubts and fears" were minor. But when he derives the American Revolution from the "fervent idealism of the immigrant Puritans"; when, having decried the French revolutionary tendency toward abstract rights, he declares of American revolutionary writing that "a yearning for absolute truth, an unbroken faith in abstract ideals, is what makes distinctly national the political utterances of the American Revolution"; when he instructs modern writers to pattern themselves upon "the simple, hopeful literature of inexperienced, renascent New England [where], for a while, the warring ideals of democracy and of excellence were once reconciled, dwelling confidently together in some early semblance of peace"; when he tells us that

100

American literature is "the story, under new conditions, of those ideals which a common language has compelled America, almost unawares, to share with England," the limitations of the Anglophile school are evident.[55] Why, then, is the book important? It is important because it is one of a series of national literary histories, including Frazier's *Literary History of India* and Douglas Hyde's *Literary History of Ireland,* a fact which led Wendell, with all his crotchets, to conceive greatly of his subject and to avoid that apologetic air which was mephitic in the common textbooks. He wrote maturely; and he assumed that his readers were mature.

If C. F. Richardson exhibits less New England parochialism than does Wendell, he seems at first glance to suffer even more deeply from the assumptions of the racial school. Not only does he solemnly begin American literature with the Mound Builders and the illiterate Indians, but he goes on to the "Saxon characteristics" first portrayed by Tacitus. One finds him comparing the Saxon mind in England and in America, declaring that American Irishmen, Germans, and Frenchmen come under the "potent influence of . . . the dominant Saxon temper," remarking on the national adoption of Saxon ethics, and even attributing American restlessness to the "more than . . . usual Saxon mania for travel." But his book is better than this. It represents a blending of Taine and of Arnold—Taine in the sociology of his problem, Arnold in his critical canon. Unlike Barrett Wendell, he sees that Boston is not the United States, but a peculiar city which "dared be radical, because it felt the weight of scholarship and social conservatism behind it." His hope for American letters is that they shall be "the literature of a cultured and genuine

101

Democracy, a sort of Saxon-Greek Renaissance in the New World." "If such a literature cannot exist and be true and grow great," he remarks, "then all the predictions of wise men from Plato to Milton, from Cicero to Victor Hugo, have been at fault." The temper of such an appraisal is judicious; it does not sink into mere sociology. Reading Richardson's critical accounts of leading American authors, one is impressed by the ease with which he moves into the current of general ideas, as when he notes that American literature "owes much of its growth to the constant and beneficial influence of such a creator, critic, and stimulating power as Channing." [56] This facility one suspects he owes to Arnold. Richardson tries to do something with American philosophical writing, and passes beyond London to Scotland, Sweden, Germany, and France to account for it. Old-fashioned, yet sound, these volumes are as close to *Geisteswissenschaft* as anything in American literary history the century produced, as will instantly appear if one compares them with Henry A. Beers's *Outline Sketch of American Literature* (1887), Francis H. Underwood's *Builders of American Literature* (1893), Henry C. Vedder's *American Writers of To-day* (1894), or any other of the genteel manuals of the time. Richardson is unfairly ignored today, for his racism is not organic like Wendell's and scarcely colors his intellectual judgments.

Greater than either Wendell or Richardson, and possibly the foremost literary historian the American problem has produced, was Moses Coit Tyler (1835–1900), whose four superb volumes are still unsurpassed, still the standard history of our first two literary centuries.[57] One great advantage which Tyler enjoyed over other literary historians was the wide, if unconscious, education life gave him for his task. A student at the University of Michigan, at Yale, and at Andover, he served as a minister in Owego and Poughkeepsie, New York; became a disciple of Henry Ward Beecher and of Dio Lewis, the advocate of calisthenics; lectured in England as a free-lance writer and speaker; and between two appointments at the University of Michigan undertook editorial writing for Beecher's *Christian Union.* Besides his work as a teacher of English, he was one of the organizers of the American Historical Association (1884); and in addition to his great literary histories, he wrote fiction of a sort, a travel book on England, a biography of Patrick Henry, and a book of biographical interpretations of Berkeley, Timothy Dwight, and Joel Barlow. Experience on the *Christian Union,* exposure to the Beecher-Tilton divorce scandal, and some political experience gave Tyler a profound disgust with the Gilded Age, which may have influenced his attitude toward the colonial and revolutionary periods. As a commentator on early American literature remarked in 1889, it expressed "the faith and joy of the early republicans in the sturdy principles of their new nation." [58] It was precisely this sense of sturdy vigor, of faith in principles, and of deep-seated happiness in seeing them develop that makes Tyler's histories of permanent worth.

Tyler was profoundly influenced by Buckle and by Sainte-Beuve. Of Buckle's *History of Civilization* he wrote that it obsessed him for weeks together. Buckle confirmed him both in a belief in progress and in the conception that the literary expression of ideas is no small force in history. Sainte-Beuve encouraged him to seek a *qualité maîtresse* in a writer, to dramatize criticism by painting a historical portrait. He found in Sainte-Beuve a law connecting crit-

icism and biography, a law which in one phase made it the
duty of a critic to "place himself at the standpoint of the
author" and in another aspect required the historian to
study both the producer and the thing produced. This was
"a law of relation between living and thinking," so that
"the conduct of phrase is part of the conduct of life"; and,
more succinctly than elsewhere, the preface to *The Literary
History of the American Revolution* expresses the mature
doctrine of Tyler, an amalgam of Buckle, Sainte-Beuve, and
twenty years of his own reflections:

> The proceedings of legislative bodies, the doings of cabinet
> ministers, and of colonial politicians, the movements of armies,
> are not here altogether disregarded, but they are here subordi-
> nated: they are mentioned, when mentioned at all, as mere ex-
> ternal incidents in connection with the ideas and the emotions
> which lay back of them. . . . We here for the most part turn
> our eyes away toward certain persons hitherto much neglected,
> in many cases wholly forgotten—towards persons who, as mere
> writers, and whether otherwise prominent or not, nourished
> the springs of great historic events by creating and shaping and
> directing public opinion during all that robust time; who, so far
> as we here regard them, wielded only spiritual weapons; who
> still illustrate, for us and for all who choose to see, the majestic
> operation of ideas, the creative and decisive play of spiritual
> forces in the development of history, in the rise and fall of na-
> tions, in the aggregation and the division of races.

As one reads the four volumes which tell the story of the
development of American writing from 1607 to the end of
the Revolution, it is difficult to realize that Tyler was without access to the great research libraries now commonly
available to mature scholars, and that the exhaustive textual labors which preceded his chapters were in a sense
pioneering jobs. No previous literary historian had insisted

upon textual accuracy in the same degree, just as no previous historian had made himself master not merely of an area of American literary history but of the coequal area of political development as well. It is not without meaning that the historian of literature came to occupy a chair of American history at Cornell or that he was one of the founders of the American Historical Association, for his masters had taught him that literary productions have a functional relationship to the issues of the times which produced them, and that to attempt a history of belles-lettres in a social vacuum, particularly a history of American literature in the colonial centuries, was to make bricks without straw.

But if Tyler was a first-class scholar and investigator, he did not lack imaginative finesse. He presents his leading characters at dramatic moments in their development— Richard Mather excommunicated by the Archbishop of York, Mather Byles ascending his pulpit amid denunciations, Francis Hopkinson meeting John Adams in Peale's studio. Possibly he owes something here to Boswell's *Johnson*, but his method is biographical (like that of Sainte-Beuve and, in a different fashion, that of Gamaliel Bradford), a method that detaches the central figure from the gray mass of dates and documents, and focuses the light of history upon significant actions and writings. Because his approach was biographical, he did not classify his writers into schools, but only into loose historical and regional groups, and it may be that this is in part the reason why his pages have outlasted more facile and more transient schematizations.

How, then, does Tyler betray his membership in the Anglophile and New England historical schools? Inasmuch as his material was mainly written by authors of British ancestry, no harm of omission followed from his belief in Saxon and Protestant superiority, and small prejudice is shown. Indeed, his sympathetic treatment of the Tory writers, who, as he roundly said, had as much love for their native land, zeal for liberty, and willingness to labor, fight, and die as had the patriots, springs in part from his Anglophilism and is part of his balance and broad good sense. But his assumptions about literary virtue are the assumptions of a school of historians who held that history is past politics—the politics of the "Saxon" world—and that writing is good in proportion as it expresses, or influences, political (that is, public) values. Tyler therefore puts a high estimate on what may be called public prose—sermons, orations, and the like—but his aesthetic interpretation in the finer sense was naïve. He knew bad workmanship when he saw it, but he did not discriminate nicely among the kinds of good workmanship found even in colonial prose. He lacked insight in judging colonial and revolutionary verse; he was blind to mysticism; he failed to estimate properly the first faint beginnings of American fiction. His judgments are, in sum, rather more like the judgments of Dr. Johnson than they are like the perceptions of Walter Pater; and though colonial writing requires more of the coarse good sense of Johnson than it does of the sensibilitist values of Pater, there is ample room for sensibility and for attaching aesthetic values in American writing to aesthetic developments in the mother country. This capacity Tyler did not have, a fact which helps to explain why Barrett Wendell tried to write the history of seventeenth- and eighteenth-century American writing in British terms. The virtue that Tyler applauds in men and writers is obvious, practical, sound; literature is a form of activism, to his mind; and though the preface I have quoted refers admiringly to the "decisive play of spiritual forces," "decisive" and "forces" are the key words rather than "spiritual" and "play." The delicate glimpses of God revealed in John Cotton or Jonathan Edwards awoke in Tyler no appropriate response. Sincerity he understands, mysticism is beyond him, and he is inclined like Hawthorne to dismiss Puritan theology as quaint, meaningless, and incredibly remote. We have to await a writer like Perry Miller to see the true complexity, the intellectual harmony, and the austere beauty of the Calvinist scheme of the universe.

And of course Tyler wrote before the fashion of economic determinism, of social and political preoccupation, and of the deep distrust of individual capacity which, in the violence of our reaction against writers like Carlyle or Froude, has altered historical scholarship. He is not so simple-minded as to believe that the Pilgrim Fathers came here for religious liberty only, but it would never occur to him to interpret New England prose as the rationalization of biological or business forces. For him New England was an absolute value; it was a way of measuring the achievement and the failure of American life, and his pen portrait of Edward Johnson is typical of the warmth and richness of his sympathy in dealing with New England men:

He was a very devout and explicit Puritan; his square, stalwart common-sense made itself felt in public and private; he had a strong taste and aptitude for military affairs; and it is significant of his soundness of brain that, amid the general frenzy of the early witchcraft excitement, he was one of the few that kept their heads cool and opposed all judicial prose-

cution of those uncomely hags that were suspected of unlaw-
ful intimacy with the devil. Had a man like this—a ship-
carpenter and farmer, unlettered, unversed in affairs, a sort
of rural alderman and militia-hero—lived anywhere else than
in New England in the seventeenth century, we should by no
means have suspected him of any inclinations toward authorship. . . . It was no ambition of authorship that prompted Edward Johnson to write his book, but an important tangible
result which could be achieved in no other way. He handled the
pen as he did the sword and the broadaxe—to accomplish
something with it.[59]

And it is perhaps significant that his most serious slips as a
scholar arose when he was dealing with the southern colonies.[60] He was more than fair with a writer like Captain
John Smith or Alsop, but somehow they were not New
England men and he did not have for them or their compeers that immediate and unspoken sympathy he had for
the northern writers.

But Tyler wrote our first great American literary history. He showed his professional descendants how important intellectual energy can be in such an enterprise,
how essential it is to have an organic idea of one's book,
how important centrality of view must always be, how essential is the fusion of critical evaluation and historical
methodology in literary history, and yet how unimportant
are bibliographical niceties, minor disputations, and foot-
notes to history, provided the work is architecturally
planned and generously executed. If he had completed a
literary history of America on the scale and in the manner
with which he began, the work might have had its Vic-
torian defects, but it would have been to the subject what
Tiraboschi is to Italian literature, and it would have prevented the creation of a thirty-year interval, during which

American literary scholarship virtually disappeared, a period, moreover, during which Tyler was wrongly honored because his subject matter was somehow recondite and insignificant.

## NOTES TO CHAPTER IV

[1] How long this tradition lingered can be illustrated from a pamphlet published at Quincy, Illinois, in 1879, by Louise Maertz, *New Method for the Study of English Literature*. This is a catechism designed to carry the student from 55 B.C to A.D. 1500. The bibliography runs: *New American Cyclopaedia*; Blair's *Lectures on Rhetoric*; Quackenbos' *Rhetoric*; the introductions to Webster's and Worcester's dictionaries; Fowler's *English Grammar*; Sismondi's *Literature of the South of Europe*; Hallam's *Literature of Europe* and his *Middle Ages*; Schlegel's *History of Literature*; Chambers' *Cyclopaedia of English Literature*; Shaw's *Outlines of English Literature*; Collier's *History of English Literature*; Taine's *History of English Literature*; Warton's *History of English Poetry*; and history books by D'Aubigné and Green. The mingling of the older, cosmopolitan spirit and rising Anglophilism is evident from this mixture of titles.

[2] Two standard studies in this Anglo-American war are by William B. Cairns, *British Criticisms of American Writings, 1783–1815*, University of Wisconsin Studies in Language and Literature, no. 1 (Madison, 1918); and *British Criticisms of American Writings, 1815–1833*, University of Wisconsin Studies in Language and Literature, no. 14 (Madison, 1922).

[3] Writing on Cooper in particular and American fiction generally in the *North American Review*, LXXIV, 147–161 (January, 1852), Francis Parkman declared that the "fair promise" of Cooper's earlier novels had failed, so had most American novelists, and "in the polite walks of literature, we find much grace and style, but very little originality of thought,—productions which might as readily be taken for the work of an Englishman as of an American. . . . The cravings of the American mind, eager as they are, are amply supplied by the copious stream of English current literature; . . . the whole

complexion of their thought is tinged with it, and by a sort of necessity they think and write at second hand. . . . In all the finer functions of thought, we are still provincial, . . . [an] intellectual dependency." Henry T. Tuckerman, reviewing Duyckinck in the same magazine in April, 1856 (LXXXII, 319–349) saw in American writing principally "the perpetuity, in our branch of the Anglo-Saxon race, of that aptitude for letters, that innate capacity for manly, graceful, true, and picturesque writing, which is an inheritance from the parent stock, the natural endowment of a people eminent for reflective, humane, free utterance. . . ." The national literature had no hope of "grand, permanent, and universally acknowledged . . . mental authority" and at basis was "thoroughly and essentially English."

[4] For example, in the 1866 edition of *Character and Characteristic Men*, Edwin P. Whipple devotes an essay to "the American mind," finding its strongest force is the Saxon-English element in its modified American form. However, the "flexible, assimilative, compromising, all-accomplished Yankee, who is neither Puritan nor Cavalier," remains central; and a queer compound of practicality and idealism develops. The essay on American literature in *American Literature and Other Papers* (Boston, 1896) seems to me far more independent in its judgment, and really operates within the framework of a history of ideas, particularly theological ones.

[5] *Battles and Leaders of the Civil War* ran serially in the *Century Magazine* from November, 1884, to April, 1888, and was published in four volumes in 1887–1888, edited by R. U. Johnson and C. C. Buel. The Lincoln work ran serially in the *Century* from November, 1886, to February, 1890, and was published in ten volumes in 1890. Both were preceded by the Scribner *Campaigns of the Civil War* (13 vols.; 1881–1883).

[6] For the general background consult John Spencer Bassett's essay, "Later Historians," *Cambridge History of American Literature*, vol. III, chap. 15; and Albert Bushnell Hart, "The American School of Historians," *International Monthly*, II, 294–322 (September, 1900). The American Historical Association was founded in 1884. The *American Historical Review* began publication in 1895.

At the first meeting of the American Historical Association, Andrew D. White read a paper entitled "On Studies in General History and the History of Civilization," in which, though he deprecated specialism and directed his argument against it, he said, "Unquestionably the number of professors devoted to historical investigation in the German universities is the great cause of the fact that Germany has surpassed other modern nations not only in special researches, but in general historical investigations; . . . this indicates the lines on which historical studies are to be best developed in our own country" (*Papers of the American Historical Association,* I [1884–1886], 25–26).

[7] Edward Channing and Albert Bushnell Hart, *Guide to the Study of American History* (Boston, 1896), pp. 1, 2.

[8] See Edward Norman Saveth, "Race and Nationalism in American Historiography: The Late Nineteenth Century," *Political Science Quarterly,* LIV(3), 421–441 (September, 1939); and Theodore Clark Smith, "The Writing of American History in America from 1884 to 1934," *American Historical Review,* XL(3), 439–449 (April, 1935).

[9] Not only were there American reprints but leading publishing houses like Longmans and Macmillan brought out British and American editions simultaneously. The curious should consult the Library of Congress cards.

[10] Edward A. Freeman, *Lectures to American Audiences* (Philadelphia, 1882), pp. 360–361.

[11] *Johns Hopkins University Register, 1881–82,* p. 41. There were six lectures with an average attendance of ninety-one, whereas James Bryce, who was also at the university, drew an average attendance of one-hundred and sixty-nine. However, President Gilman had insisted that Freeman should "talk informally," not lecture, and the ninety-one were in fact a kind of magnified graduate seminar.

[12] Freeman, *American Institutional History,* p. 19. Freeman's rather strained analogy is with the Romance cantons of Switzerland. Most of his monograph was reprinted from his essay, "Impressions of America," which had appeared in the *Fortnightly Review,* August and September, 1882. As for Herbert B. Adams' enthusiasm for the racial theory see *Herbert B. Adams: Tributes of Friends* (Baltimore, 1902), particularly the sketch by Richard T. Ely; and *Historical Scholarship in the United States, 1876–1901, as revealed in the correspondence of Herbert B. Adams,* ed. W. Stull Holt, "Johns Hopkins University Studies in Historical and Political Science," series LVI, no. 4 (Baltimore, 1938).

[13] Channing-Hart, pp. 3–4.

[14] The standard work is, of course, Lois Kimball Mathews, *The Expansion of New England* (Boston, 1909). See, particularly, chapters 6–10. This admirable monograph extends only to 1865, and

though it does not ignore such cultural elements as church, school, and books, is mainly interested in political, economic, and sociological factors. Howard Allen Bridgman, *New England in the Life of the World* (Boston, 1920), is uncritical and unsystematic, but in some ways throws more light on the cultural problem than does Mathews.

[15] See *Collections and Researches made by the Michigan Pioneer and Historical Society*, XXVIII (Lansing, 1900), 204–205, for the full text.

[16] Quoted in Mathews, p. 169.

[17] *Literary Friends and Acquaintances* (New York, 1900), p. 3.

[18] An amusing comment on New Englandism is to be found in *The Booklovers Reading Club Hand-Book to Accompany the Reading Course entitled Studies in American Literary Life* (Philadelphia, 1901), which includes an essay by Lewis E. Gates of Harvard on how to read and one by Barrett Wendell on his own book. Frederic W. Speirs, the director, prefaces the handbook with this "Word": "A university professor of literature who saw the proof-sheets of this handbook remarked with just a faint note of sarcasm in his voice, 'New England is well represented in your course.' The same thought will doubtless enter the minds of many readers. . . . Two of the three books we furnish are the publications of New England men. Two of the three papers printed in the hand-book are written by Harvard professors; and the third is the production of a Boston littérateur. The editorial notes were contributed by a professor of literature [Pattee] in a Pennsylvania college, but he is by birth and education a New England man. . . . The overwhelming representation of New England was quite intentional. We sought the best available books and articles . . ." (pp. 15–16).

[19] Charles F. Richardson, *American Literature, 1607–1885* (student edition, 2 vols. in 1; New York, 1886–1888), II, 403–404 ("fact and fancy were mingled by the nervously impatient author, in the proportion desired by his immediate public"); Barrett Wendell, *A Literary History of America* (New York, 1900), p. 229 ("Herman Melville, with his books about the South Seas . . . began a career of literary promise, which never came to fruition").

[20] Wendell, p. 527.

[21] Richardson, I, viii.

[22] See the sketch of Richardson's life in the *Dictionary of American Biography*.

[23] On this general subject see Morgan Callaway, Jr., *Historic Study of the Mother-Tongue in the United States: A Survey of the Past,* "University of Texas Studies in English," no. 5 (1925); Francis A. March, "Recollections of Language Teaching," *Publications of the Modern Language Association,* VIII (n.s. I), xix–xxii (1893); J. M. Garnett, "The Study of the Anglo-Saxon Language and Literature," *Addresses and Journal of Proceedings of the National Educational Association* (1876), pp. 141–156; J. B. Henneman, "The Study of English in the South," *Sewanee Review,* II(2), 180–197 (February, 1894). On the whole problem of replacing the classics by one or another branch of modern philology, the essays collected in *Twentieth Century Modern Language Teaching: Sources and Readings,* ed. Maxim Newark (New York, 1948), are suggestive.

[24] Noah Porter, *American Colleges and the American Public* (new ed.; New York, 1878), particularly the first two chapters. Porter stoutly maintained that "the American Colleges have been from the first and uniformly schools of classical study and learning" (p. 39) and should remain so.

[25] March, p. xxi.

[26] Garnett, p. 142.

[27] G. Stanley Hall, *How to Teach Reading and What to Read in School* (Boston, 1886), p. 35. "The end in selecting stated school reading should be first and chiefly a moral one." Almost all the authorities he cites on the psychology of teaching are German.

[28] L. Sears, "The Study of Anglo-Saxon," *57th Annual Meeting of the American Institute of Instruction* (Boston, 1887), pp. 76, 79, 83.

[29] James M. Garnett, "The Position of Old English in a General Education," *Paper before the Virginia Association for the Advancement of Higher Education* (Virginia Beach, July 10, 1889) in the *Academy,* V, 112–123 (March, 1890).

[30] Morton W. Easton, "Comparative Grammar," *The Academy: A Journal of Secondary Education,* IV(9), 494–495 (December, 1889).

[31] Garnett, p. 120.

[32] F. A. Barbour, "Anglo-Saxon in the High School," *Academy,* V(3), 166 (April, 1890). See also John S. Hart (then principal of the Philadelphia High School), "On the Study of the Anglo-Saxon Language," *Proceedings of the Fourth Session of the American Association for the Advancement of Education* (1855), an early bit of

propaganda which touched off a spirited debate, not merely about classical and modern languages, but also about the proper training of teachers.

[33] T. W. Hunt, "The Place of English in the College Curriculum," *Transactions of the Modern Language Association,* I, 119 (1884–1885).

[34] These essays were cumulated in a book. See William Morton Payne, ed., *English in American Universities. By Professors in the English Departments of Twenty Representative Institutions* (Boston, 1895).

[35] In the January, 1891, issue of the *Academy,* V(10), 513–528 (January, 1891), S. Thurber of Boston outlines a scheme of study for teachers of English, philological in scope. The accompanying bibliography ignores American writing.

[36] Hunt, p. 125. Hunt proved to his own satisfaction that in the eighties "men are often appointed to English chairs apparently for no other reason than that they are able to speak the language grammatically and have a general society knowledge of the literature" (p. 119), and his program of reform had philology as its backbone.

[37] See, for example, J. Earle, "The Study of English," *Forum,* XIII(1), 75–84 (March, 1892), based on returns from the colleges, which presents the view that comparative philology, scientific grammar, and the like studies will improve the vocabulary of the student.

[38] George R. Carpenter, Franklin T. Baker, and Fred N. Scott, *The Teaching of English in the Elementary and Secondary School* (New York, 1910), p. 215.

[39] Irked by Woodrow Wilson's famous essay on "Mere Literature," Albert S. Cook, in *The Higher Study of English* (Boston, 1906), took all literary knowledge as "the province of English philology" in the opening essay of that volume.

[40] Payne, p. 27.

[41] Cook, p. 57.

[42] Hunt, p. 129.

[43] Francis H. Underwood, *English Literature and Its Place in Popular Education. An Essay read before the National Teachers' Association, Boston, August, 1872* (Boston and New York, 1879), p. 12. But even Underwood propagandized for racism: ". . . The body of English literature . . . contains more of grandeur and beauty, more of pathos and wit, more of humor (a quality in some respects peculiar to our race), more of fervid oratory, and more of noble history, than the stores of the classic languages combined."

[44] See the interesting observations on this topic by Professor Jay Hubbell, "The Decay of the Provinces," *Sewanee Review*, XXXV(4), 473–487 (October, 1927). He quotes with humorous approval the famous line that there are "only eastern windows in the houses of the Brahmins."

[45] *North American Review*, CCXLVII(1), 8–9 (Spring, 1939).

[46] Ferner Nuhn, "Teaching American Literature in American Colleges," *American Mercury*, XIII(51), 328–331 (March, 1928). He found an average of one out of eleven courses in the English departments was devoted to American literature at the undergraduate level; and about one out of thirteen at the graduate level. At Harvard in 1926–1927 thirteen doctoral dissertations were accepted, none of them in American literature.

[47] John Pierpont, *The American First Class Book* (Boston, 1823), was "got up" for the Boston public schools; and this done, the contents of the readers were sometimes arranged for local or regional needs.

[48] When one considers that Emerson's essays were lectures before they were essays, and remembers how much of Lowell, Bryant, Channing, Margaret Fuller, and other writers was originally planned as public discourse, the oral quality of American style is explained.

[49] *English in Secondary Schools: Report of a Committee of the Massachusetts Teachers Association*, December 1, 1888, p. 3. This is apparently a reprint from an article in the *Academy*.

[50] Carpenter, Baker, and Scott, pp. 310 ff.

[51] Henry S. Pancoast, *An Introduction to American Literature* (New York, 1898), p. 2.

[52] *Ibid.*, p. 6. The whole passage is fascinating: "The United States is by no means the only country in which the civilization and literature of England are being carried forward under new conditions. For centuries, and especially during the last one hundred and fifty years, the English people have been building outside of the narrow limits of their island a great Empire that is now ninety-one times as large as the mother-land. The English flag waves over tropic India and among Canadian forests; in Australasia, in the distant Southern ocean, the English have raised up a rich, progressive, and powerful state; in half-mapped Africa is the wonderful spectacle of this widening English rule. It is not English rule merely, it is England herself, her Christian civilization, her institutions, her law, her language, and her literature that are thus reaching out to the ends of the world. To-day nearly four hundred millions of people, of widely different

race, language, and inheritance, acknowledge her supremacy, while to more than one hundred millions, including the people of the United States, her language and her literature are native and inherited possessions. Such a fact marks an epoch, not only in the history of the English people, but in the history of English literature. This 'expansion of England' means also the expansion of English literature; it means that the English genius, which has been revealing itself through literature for more than twelve hundred years, has won for its use fresh materials for literary art by coming into contact with new and infinitely varied life. Our true place in literary history is as one of the literatures of this greater England" (pp. 5–6). Somehow I can only think of Halford John Mackinder's remark (*Democratic Ideals and Reality,* New York, 1942, p. 147) that the British and the Germans took seats in express trains on the same line, but in opposite directions.

[53] Mary Fisher, *A General Survey of American Literature* (Chicago, 1899), p. 12.

[54] John Nichol, *American Literature: An Historical Sketch, 1620–1880* (Edinburgh, 1882). Why this excellent book, which began as a series of lectures in Edinburgh in 1861 and was constantly enriched by continuing study, is neglected I do not know. The introductory chapter is an implicit rebuke to chauvinism and to Anglophilism; and the chapter on American humorists is penetrating. His discussion of the general characteristics of contemporary American writing is on pp. 446–448. See, in this connection, an interesting review article on this book in the *Athenaeum,* I(2882), 79–81 (January 20, 1883).

[55] Wendell, pp. 29, 524, 525, 530, 521. Wendell's book was widely reviewed, stress being laid on racial inheritances common to the two nations. See, for a typical instance, G. H. Powell, "The Mind of America," *Contemporary,* LXXXII, 111–125 (July, 1902), where one reads that the United States must take up her share of the "Anglo-Saxon burden," that America and the British Empire represent a "great Democratic Alliance," and that we must abandon isolationism.

[56] Richardson, I, 22, 52, 55, 61–62, 288–292.

[57] On Tyler, see Jessica Tyler Austen, *Moses Coit Tyler: Selections from his Letters and Diaries* (New York, 1911); and H. M. Jones, *The Life of Moses Coit Tyler,* based on an unpublished dissertation by T. E. Casady (Ann Arbor, 1933).

[58] From an unsigned review article in the *Overland Monthly,* n.s.

XIV, 549–556 (1889) commenting on the Stedman-Hutchinson *Library of American Literature.*

[59] *History of American Literature,* I, 137–138.

[60] See Jones, *Tyler,* pp. 194 ff. On the other hand, his *Patrick Henry* is standard and sympathetic.

# V

# "A Usable Past"

THE INTERPLAY of literary history and literary criticism is or should be constant, influential ideas developed in one field of interpretation having also important effects in the other. If, for example, a Coleridge propounds the doctrine that the unity of a work of art is organic rather than mechanical, literary historians come by and by to interpret artistic development in analogus terms, as does Oliver Elton in his *Survey of English Literature*. If, on the other hand, historians underline the truth that even genius owes something to its predecessors, something to its apprenticeship, and something to its contemporaries, Shakespearean criticism is compelled to abandon its romantic image of self-willed and changeless perfection and to estimate the poet in terms of his development, the conditions of his craft, and the conventions and limitations of his time. Whenever literary history abandons evaluation, it becomes archaeological and dry; whenever literary criticism neglects history, it grows absolute and inhuman.

As we approach the wonderful efflorescence of scholarship and criticism in American literature of the twentieth century, we must perforce keep this Janus-faced principle steadily in view. It is our main clue to understanding the development of scholarship in the American field during the last fifty years. The central effort in this development has been the attempt to find a historical answer to a critical question. That question is: How can the United States discover a usable past? The phrase was coined by Van Wyck Brooks, a fact of some significance for the interplay of history and criticism, since, even amid the iconoclasms of his earlier volumes, Mr. Brooks wrote like an American Arnold, and in his later, more historical works, though his style is no longer Arnoldian, his standards have become traditional and conservative. Moreover, the problem of a usable past has a double aspect. In one way, it is simply a variant of the oldest question in American literary history; namely, shall American letters be shaggy, unique, and powerful, or shall they participate in western tradition and benefit by the experience of older nations? In another sense, however, the query: How shall the United States find a usable past? marks a dramatic transvaluation of values. The governing philosophy of our culture before 1914 has been less concerned with the past than with the future. Its anxiety has been to show that republican institutions necessarily produce a virtuous culture. But the new question implied that the utopian view of a novel literature born of unique institutions had fled; that the duty of educated men was now to turn to the past, there to discover the rooted strength and classic formularies of the American ideal; and that, in an age of alternate bewilderment and power, we had lost confidence in the seminal virtues of democracy.

Dates are arbitrary; periods overlap; generalizations prove fallacious. It is convenient to date the latest phase of American literary history from 1913, when John Macy

119

published his *Spirit of American Literature*, the first book wholly devoted to literary history springing from the "new spirit" in literary criticism. Mr. Macy's stiletto can be measured from a remark in his *Critical Game*, where, reviewing the *Collected Essays* of George Edward Woodberry, he writes that Woodberry "became the last of the Lowells instead of the first of the Woodberrys"—is, in other words, "out of date because he did not gear with his own times." [1] The usual handbooks and histories of American literature, Macy declared in his treatise, "pay too much attention to doubly dead worthies, whose books are not interesting, and miss or but timidly acknowledge contemporary excellence." Scholars, he flatly said, are "intellectually a poor generation"; and he insisted that the classic American writers "turn their backs on life" and "miss its intensities," that after the Civil War our literary imagination was "almost sterile," and that we would no longer put up with names which "persist by the inertia of reputation." [2] This dictum ignored, diminished, or dethroned Edwards, Bryant, Longfellow, Whittier, Poe, Holmes, Lowell, and Howells, and exalted Thoreau, Melville, Whitman, Twain, and William James.

## 2

However radical Macy may have seemed to contemporary reviewers, literary history seldom admits of revolution, and the storm had been long preparing. Between 1880 and World War I hundreds of articles and an impressive library of books by Americans (and others) debated the problem of the national letters. The old question, partly of fact,

partly of casuistry, whether American production was anything more than a part of English literature continued to be
posed; and if it has since expired, its death is due rather to
futility than to persuasion and conviction. In general, the
doctrine that American literature (with American culture)
was, and must be, a failure except as a local branch of
British literature was a constant theme. Ostensibly talking
about Salem and Concord in his book on Hawthorne, but
also with an eye on the Gilded Age, Henry James had
complained in 1879 that nature in America is "crude and
immature," society "thinly-composed," the country lacking
in the "complex social machinery" needed "to set a writer
in motion"; [3] and the inference that American topics,
American genius, and American culture were inevitably
barren was extensively discussed. In 1883 Kinahan Cornwallis could find "no rising generation of American
authors"; [4] in 1888 Charles Eliot Norton opined that
America had made no intellectual contribution to the world
corresponding to her material contributions, culture being
taught only for purposes of gaining a livelihood; [5] and in
1894 Henry C. Vedder could find "very little that makes
any pretence of being serious criticism of the writers of our
own day," and "no poet who was poet and nothing else,"
but only "an unusual proportion of clever men." [6] Five
years later Hamilton Wright Mabie declared that "our
literature for two decades has not made a very deep impression on the imagination of the country and has not
deeply affected its character because, for the most part it
has lacked depth of feeling and profound seriousness." [7]
Reviewing Stedman's *American Anthology,* Oscar L.
Triggs in 1901 reached the conclusion that the volume "be-

tokens the inadequacy of poetic literature to sustain a large and vigorous modern national life," [8] and in the next decade a variety of commentators reached conclusions equally dispiriting. For example,

Literature was becoming only the echo of an idle dilettant-ism. . . .

In our new and more expansive patriotism which prevails with us we prefer our own rubbish to the rubbish that we used to plunder the English of.

Most American writers have not lived enough, have not experienced enough, and their spiritual life is shallow.

It has become impossible to determine whether art, at its best estate, can flourish in the atmosphere of democracy and irreligion, or whether what may remain of it is not a survival from some remote past, a leftover achievement of many generations.

Neither in quantity nor in quality can the poetry so far produced by this nation be held commensurate to its greatness in other fields. [9]

Writing in the *Bookman* in 1906, James H. Collins divided American writing into the "strenuous," the "fashionplate," the "cosmic monotone," and the "optimo-platitudinous," and opined that "nowhere else . . . has such a volume of writing become 'standardized.' " [10] In the *Dial* for 1910, Charles Leonard Moore could see little ahead except poverty and dulness,[11] and in 1912 the *Forum* printed a striking article by Hanna Astrup Larsen entitled "The Cowardice of American Literature," containing such dicta as: "American fiction until recently was so moral as to be immoral, because it has no place for truth"; and "Puritanism is not so fatal to art as is the American flippancy, which we flatter ourselves by calling the national sense of humor." [12]

Such were characteristic indictments. Defenders of an American cultural tradition developed three positions, partially interrelated; they might admit the charges as proof that provincialism was inevitable and so reconcile themselves to British superiority; they might partially admit the indictment and yet, through the rationalization of values in the genteel tradition, find an encouraging amount of "idealism" in American letters; or they might flatly deny the allegation and set up the theory that American literature was in fact fulfilling the promise of independent life in the context of republican institutions. It is convenient to glance at these theories in reverse order, since their discussion creates the background of the shift in literary history we are about to discuss.

In 1881 Whitman's "Poetry of the Future" had expressed his belief that American literature must be unique and bold, a position reaffirmed in 1891,[13] and a small army of critics discovered corroborative evidence of literary independence. Thus in a long, thoughtful article on "The Native Element in American Fiction" printed in the *Century* in 1883, James Herbert Morse, after reviewing the development from Charles Brockden Brown to the present, concluded that the American muse was "clothed in the new garments of the national life."

A life which has mastered a continent and developed its enormous resources, which has handled successfully so much of the capital of Europe, which has freed a nation of slaves and already partly digested a small empire of the difficult subjects of European mismanagement, which has survived a war of almost incredibly disintegrating properties, and which yet finds itself no worse in the blood than England was eighteen years after Waterloo—such a life is rich enough to meet the largest demands of the novelist.[14]

America, said Julian Hawthorne on the same theme, is "a new departure in history," so that "he who fears Europe is a less respectable snob than he who studies it." [15] Howells and James, thought Balestier in 1886, have started a new era, so that American literature will not be a supplement to English literature but will stand alone.[16] "The American artist," wrote Garland a little later, "must grow out of American conditions and reflect them without deprecatory shrug or spoken apology." [17] American development, according to B. W. Wells in 1897, "is independent, and so is contributing an important, perhaps an essential, part to the growth of distinctly national literature." [18] In 1900, William P. Trent analyzed literary trends in all fields of American writing, declaring that, at any rate, American writers had not fallen down as American politicians had fallen down; [19] Howells said we have always had "adequate expression," [20] and in 1906, writing in the *Arena*, Winifred Webb, answering Gertrude Atherton, bade American writers glory in the fact that they are middle class, for we are just coming into "national self-consciousness." [21] Obviously, such pronunciamentos did not differ greatly from those of a century before.[22] The important fact is the increasing number of voices singing the chorus of literary independence.

Corroboration of these general views was derived from two broad areas: regionalism, and the development of fiction. The general rationalization of regionalism can be clearly studied in an editorial in the *Independent* for 1902, the writer of which advised critics to give up searching after a "national" letters, since the diversity of the country made a single literature impossible: "We are spellbound in our own sections by different climates, conditions and

standards of living, and until time welds this great nation
into as homogeneous a whole as England has enjoyed for
many centuries we must despair. . . ." In the rich development of a sectional spirit the editor saw hope—New England had led the way, the West was about to follow
(despite a "subconscious fatalism"), and the South, though
limited by prejudice and "still posing, old, desolate and
magnificently proud," would in time make its brilliant contribution.[23] The editorial was but rephrasing Garland's
theory that "the history of American literature is the history
of provincialism slowly becoming less all-pervasive—the
history of the slow development of a distinctive utterance"[24] in the form of that Veritism, local yet universal,
for which he stood. Of course, no regionalist was satisfied
with present productions—Norris thought that "Western
literature" was "a cult indulged in by certain well-bred
gentlemen in New England who looked eastward . . . for
their inspiration," the "resolute deeds" of their own countrymen being left to "nameless hacks"[25]—but more characteristic was the faith of Herbert Bashford in the "spirit of
freedom" in all western authors, and in the ability of grandi-
ose scenery to produce "inspiration":[26]

whether or not they [authors] be particularly observant, this
close association with natural scenery leads to a sensitive and
emotional organism that most frequently finds expression in the
form of verse, the abundant production of which by Califor-
nians is becoming more and more apparent to the editorial observation.[27]

The South indignantly repudiated Woodberry's theory that
it had been, and was likely to remain, provincial and barren;[28] it preferred to believe, even as early as 1900, that
"work is being done in the South to-day in almost every

field of literature—not, indeed, great work, but worthy work"; [29] and when the *Library of Southern Literature* (1907–1909) appeared in fifteen fat volumes, it learned with pride that the purpose of this cyclopedia was not "sectional glorification" but "national enrichment." Was not the South "the richest in romanticism and idealism, in tragedy and suffering, and in pride of region and love of home"? "The literary barrenness of the South has been overstated, and its contributions to American literature undervalued, both as to quantity and quality." The South had produced a new literature, marked by "new energy, new freedom and self-analysis, and descriptive power." [30] At least there were many who thought so. As for New England, the general attitude was that its day was over. That the effects of the Civil War, which could be traced in southern poetry,[31] left no similar traces on New England literature was apparently a general assumption.

The second great support for the doctrine that American literature had achieved its independence (or was about to) was the extraordinary interest in the writing and theory of fiction displayed in the last third of the nineteenth century. Here the great central topic was that strange myth, the Great American Novel. As a close student of this queer theme has observed, "To the impartial reader of the periodicals of the age it must have seemed that those Americans who were not actually attempting to write the great American novel, were busy offering hints to those who were," [32] nor did the excitement wholly die down until the new century had dawned. As late as 1909 so good a critic as H. W. Boynton found it necessary to assure readers of the *Nation* that he had ceased to look for the Great American Novel, the reason being that there were "so many excellent novels" being written in the United States,[33] and it was, indeed, to the great library of fiction produced in the eighties and nineties that apologists for the American muse proudly referred. When the Great American Novel was not in question, a working relation was alleged between American fiction and realism; or if not that, between American history and the glories of American historical romance.[34] There were, of course, doubters. American novelists "cater to the ladies," said Boyesen in 1887. *The* American novel "has never been written, and never will be until centuries have passed away," wrote M. H. Lawless in 1890. It had not appeared by 1904, if a contributor to the *Bookman* was to be believed; the novel was a passing form, according to a critic of 1906; it had no social background in 1912; and critical comparisons between British and American fiction usually admitted the superiority of the Old World.[35] But doubt was swept away as James, Howells, Julian Hawthorne, George Pellew, C. Alphonso Smith, Arnold Bennett, Robert Herrick, and others dwelt upon the range and richness of the form, the delight of its technical excellence, and the important functional relation between the art of fiction and the changing facets of American society. Herrick summed up twenty-five years of debate when he wrote in 1914:

Our literature will not continue to ignore for another twenty years the daily lives and spiritual experiences of four-fifths of the people, nor of all those of stranger blood whom fate has placed in our social system. In this way, I foresee our novels coming to include the larger interests. . . . [The novelist] should represent men and women as they are in the struggle of modern life, actuated by the serious ideas and ideals of their time, not solely as sentimental puppets preoccupied with getting married.[36]

To those who could not accept the more roseate view of American literary achievement members of the genteel tradition offered the suggestion that the national letters, if they were still in a process of becoming, were nevertheless expressive, however imperfectly, of that idealism on which the republic depended for its spiritual life. Time has unfortunately dealt more harshly with the genteel critics than they merit, but a book like Stedman's *Poets of America* (1885), with its excellent discussion of the virtues and defects of Whitman, or a theoretical volume like Hamilton Wright Mabie's *Books and Culture* (1896) by no means deserves the irony it drew from Santayana. Mabie's theory is not original with him, but it is intelligently presented. Opposed to mechanism in thought and morals, he is a vitalist, and the truth of a vitalistic theory of life is known to him by meditation and imaginative insight, guided by great books—Shakespeare, Goethe, the Greeks. In the light of this revelation of universal values let the individual learn to live worthily as a member of a great racial tradition and in his private capacity; let him seek complete and balanced realization of self and let him work for social idealism. Art is "a finality both of experience and of thought"; idealism "is the application of the imagination to realities"; and the idealistic movement is "the hope and safeguard of society." [37] There were those who thought the national letters, however imperfect, were at least headed in the right direction and who, picking up the hypothesis of Madame de Staël and others, discovered a working relation among idealism, literature, and the liberal state.

"It is in the unfolding of higher and nobler ideas of living, as connected with the development of democracy, that the future of American literature will find its truest and widest influence and scope," one magazine declared in 1881,[38] and a considerable discussion rang changes on this theme. Somewhat surprisingly in view of his legend, Richard Watson Gilder saw profit in American realism because it moved in this general direction.[39] In the preface to his *American Anthology* (1900) Stedman stated that the republic was founded upon idealism, and that poets rather than practical men had kept idealism alive; and the volume drew from the *Dial* commendatory comment—American poetry has kept the "torch of our national idealism aflame."[40] The *Outlook* in 1902 discovered in American literature a "fusion of a keen perception of fact and a lofty and even rarified kind of idealism,"[41] the latter, alas! sometimes veiled, and in 1912 Benjamin A. Heydrick declared that

In general, the view of American life presented by poetry is more hopeful, more encouraging, than that found in fiction or the drama. Our poets see the evils and dangers in our national life, but they are not for a moment doubtful of the ultimate result.[42]

It was, of course, possible to twist the idealist position into a defense of literary reaction, as did Robert Underwood Johnson in 1912 when he wrote:

If writing is to be an art . . . we shall need all the conservative forces we can command: such as respect for learning, the steeping of one's self in good literature, and the cultivation of nobility and dignity of view as against the vulgarity of standard that places the accent of contempt upon 'highbrows' . . . [43]

but the more usual theory was set forth by Archibald Henderson in 1913:

It is to that same power of a risen people, awakened in the intellectual as in the political realm, that we must look for the realization of a new age of literary culture. . . . Today the whole world [and especially the United States] is one vast democracy—the democracy of the spirit.[44]

And the year before World War I began, Ephraim D. Adams lectured at Yale on "The Power of Ideals in American History." [45] Quotation could be indefinitely multiplied, but enough has been shown to demonstrate the strength of the tradition that American literature was filled with "idealism" and that its particular variety of idealism, whatever the artistic demerits might appear, was a necessary product of democracy.[46]

But the genteel idealists were caught in a dilemma, as the Anglophiles were quick to see. You could not consistently admit that American literature was full of defects and at the same time argue that it was a glorious expression of national idealism. Commenting on Whitman in 1881, one writer dryly remarked that "American ideas suitable to poetry are not so numerous or so definite that a very large body of poetry can be expected of them at once"; [47] and if you doubted as a critic that "any purely American novel will ever seem quite so good as its best English or French competitor," [48] it seemed wiser to give up the argument that the national letters bear "emphatic witness to the purity, the spirituality, and the artistic instinct of the American mind," [49] in favor of the theory that literature in the United States, impoverished by being cut off from Europe,[50] must remain indefinitely a branch of British culture. "The fine work of the poets of America shows, not that there is any probability that a national poetry will ever be developed in America, but that English poetry can be enriched by English writers born on American soil. . . ."[51] A fundamental unity of the British and Ameri-

can peoples, thought one reviewer, was revealed in the
Wendell history; [52] and Brander Matthews said roundly
that "the relation between the British branch of English
literature and the American branch must ever be intimate;
and there is disadvantage in considering the one without
keeping the other in mind always." [53] In 1914 Louis How
declared that American literature was without greatness,
having tried "culture and patient imitation" and "anarchy
and impatient originality" and found them both wanting;
that same year H. Houston Peckham admitted the Americans "have *not* had nearly so good a chance as the mother
country to produce great books." And, blandly quoting as
characteristic American work,

> Sassafras, oh sassafras,
>   Thou art the stuff for me
> And in the spring I love to sing,
>   Sweet sassafras, of thee,

John L. McMaster muttered: better fifty words on Europe
than a sonnet on Broadway.[54] Variants on the Anglophile
explanation included (as accounting for American weakness) the absence of good classical teaching [55] and the
theory that American literature was sharing the same weakness as that of European letters, American opinion to the
contrary notwithstanding. All modern literature seems to
the conservatives to be feeble.

The discussion was confused, the details confusing, but
it is possible to sum up the drift of thought in a series of
questions. Was our literature directly conditioned by, and
expressive of, democratic values? Were these primarily
social and political, or were they intellectual and cultural?
If they were the latter, did we not lack that stratified society without which, it was alleged, a cultured literature

131

could not exist? Was realism a fatal gift from decadent Europe; or was it the instrument on which to seize if we were to forge an art expressing the American way of life? Was not our literature bound to be regional, parochial, even local and assuredly second-rate; or was it somehow to produce a mighty masterpiece to be known as the Great American Novel? Did we not lack craftsmanship? Scholarship? Genius? Was not the commercial spirit of the republic now, and always, the enemy of art? Was not the tyranny of women over literature reprehensible? And always the ancient theme emerged: we are a young country engaged in subduing a continent, dedicated to material prosperity, impatient of the finer things. Such were leading questions in the magazine debate.

3

If we turn to the books, which had, at least in intention, a more perdurable value, we find that the manufacture of school texts of the Anglophile order steadily continued. Most of these did not rise above the intellectual level of the books of this sort described in the previous chapter; and not until the publication of William B. Cairns's *History of American Literature* (1912) did the "college literary history" volume achieve scholarly repute—if we except certain titles about to be discussed. On another level and for another audience, general readers were furnished with anecdotal, gossipy, or "cultural" volumes such as Donald Grant Mitchell's *American Lands and Letters* (1897) and its sequel, M. A. DeWolfe Howe's *American Bookmen* (1898), or Richard Burton's *Literary Leaders of America* (1903), essays which justify the reproaches heaped upon the genteel tradition. Fortunately, literary history rose above this sort of thing.

Certain writers between 1880 and 1913 stand out from the gray monotony either because of the freshness of their insight or because of the intellectual courage with which they generalize on American literature. Though Henry James did not pretend to be a literary historian, his perceptions were always interesting, and in *Partial Portraits* (1888) he shrewdly noted that the very plainness of a "god-fearing, practical society" in Emerson's time and after, a society living, as it were, within "undecorated walls," necessarily showered special distinction upon anybody having a "connection with literature." "There is no country in which it is more freely admitted to be a distinction—*the* distinction; or in which so many persons have become eminent for showing it even in a slight degree." [56] And if James's remarks are a good prologue to critical honesty, the publication of the ten solid volumes of *A Library of American Literature* (1888–1890) edited by Stedman and Ellen Mackay Hutchinson, suggested a variety of problems for the learned, even though the cyclopedia was intended for popular consumption. [57]

A few literary histories in the proper sense rose above mediocrity. In her *American Literature* (1897) Katharine Lee Bates sought to illumine literary history by tracing (however faintly) the development of painting, sculpture, and music in this country. Her curious statement that "American men of letters are too busy nowadays to achieve their best" indicates a failure of insight, and her declaration that we are a people "practically without folk-songs" rings quaintly nowadays; yet, though she produced merely another Anglophile volume, her efforts show at least the stir of change.[58] So, too, does Edwin Percy Whipple's *American Literature and Other Papers* (1896), in which that neglected critic anticipates Herbert Schneider and Perry Miller by assuming that American views of God have much to do with our philosophy of art.[59] Pattee's early volume, *A History of American Literature with a View of the Fundamental Principles Underlying Its Development* (1896) was a school text which announced an ambitious program strongly influenced by Taine, for the "fundamental principles" include race, environment, epoch, and personality. Unfortunately, they had small effect upon the book.[60] In his *History of American Literature* (1903) William P. Trent vaguely adopted an evolutionary theory and had the temerity to say:

> Leaving out the names of Milton and Baxter, of Bunyan, in his masterpieces, and a few other writers, we find that the great body of English Puritanism did little or nothing for English poetry in the seventeenth century, and not a great deal for English prose. Indeed, it is possible to maintain that Puritanism in New England during this period reached a higher level of literary excellence, such as it was, than it did in England apart from the manifestation of two very great literary geniuses, and that if every emigrant to New England had remained in Old England the roll of the British poets would probably not have been lengthened materially.[61]

Finally, though it is not formally a literary history, W. C. Brownell's *American Prose Masters* (1901) must long remain one of the finest commentaries we have on nineteenth-century American prose from Cooper to Henry James, albeit modern criticism wonders at his omission of Melville.[62]

The common assumption before 1913 among literary historians was that American literature had been and must continue to be a provincial branch of British culture. However, two books from the period brilliantly dispute this notion. The first of these, entitled *The Philosophy of American Literature* (1890), is by Greenough White, who managed to distill more original thinking into sixty-six pages than had any previous student of this complicated problem. The second, *America in Literature* (1903), by George E. Woodberry, more orthodox in tone, nevertheless insists that our dependence has not been upon Great Britain but upon Europe as a totality, a view natural enough in a man who taught comparative literature at Columbia University. But let us begin with White.

American literature, says this author, is no "mere pallid reflection of literary fashions beyond the Atlantic," since, he argues,

our literature has really developed with admirable freedom, energy, and completeness. It has not been dwarfed by those influences nor have its epochs been cut short by those political and international complications that have so often thwarted mental progress in other lands. It shows the natural unfolding of intellect freed from old-world trammels, yet limited by the necessities of practical life. Its growth has been dynamic.

In thus denying the provincial position of American writing, White turned the Anglophile argument neatly against itself: were American literature a mere echo of Great Britain, "there could be no more telling criticism of American intellect; no clearer proof could be afforded of a supposed degeneracy of the race when transplanted to American soil, and of the worthlessness of our civilization. . . ." Such an admission was, of course, precisely the admission Anglophilism could not make. And White also denied the "idealism" commonly attributed to the Puritans of

New England by historians of the Anglophile persuasion. Anticipating a good many recent writers, he found
that American Puritanism was a decaying stage of culture, "decidedly Manichaean." Satan had more power
in America than God. "Degrading imaginations, pruriency,
and puerile superstitions resulted. . . . The diseased mind
of the Puritan found signs and wonders in changes of the
weather. . . ." "The Puritans quoted freely from Greek
and Roman authors, yet despised them as heathens." "As
regards the sectaries with whom they came in contact, the
Puritans seem to have been incapable of distinguishing
between human beings and doctrines." White is clearly
wrong in denying Puritan interest in science and the arts
(as he does), just as he is mistaken in other points of his
essay, but a quarter of a century before Macy, Van Wyck
Brooks, H. L. Mencken, and Ludwig Lewisohn, he was at-
tacking conventional valuations of colonial culture. Moreover, his book is studded with valuable *aperçus*, as when
he writes that Frisbie's review of Adam Smith's *Theory of
the Moral Sentiments* in 1819 is one of the "memorable
events in the history of American literature," or notes the
profound importance in the period 1820–1840 of the re-
vival of interest in the literature and art of Italy and Spain,
and of the decades 1840–1860, which deepened the appeal
of the thought of Germany and of ancient Greece to American writers.[63] If some of his ideas are extravagant, other
valuable ones even yet remain neglected by historians.

White's essay was but a sketch; Woodberry's treatise is a
formal book, resting on racial theories that are outmoded
and on a Platonic doctrine of beauty not all can accept.
The originality of the work consists in the author's quiet
insistence upon the insufficiency of the Anglophile theory

of American development. Our dependence, he argues, has been upon Europe, not upon the British Isles.

It is to be observed that this connection with the Continent, so natural, so continuous, so radiant with what it gave to us, was one through culture, either literary or artistic, and not one through action; it was the past of these lands, not their present —the antiquity, learning, and sentiment of their past, not the romanticism of their still vital present—that attracted the American interest . . .

he says in one place, and in another:

This ancient and rich literary past was the source of our artistic tradition, and the sense of its dignity and preciousness was always great in the scholars among our writers, and nearly all of them were scholarly men. They lived habitually in it, they learned from it, they emulated its works. In other words, they had the academic mind. They were but partly naturalized even in the country in which they were born; they were sharers in the cosmopolitanism of the modern world, and it was forced on them by the state of American culture.

Woodberry was aware that such writers exhibit "something that may be called the timidity of the scholar" and agrees that Lowell is a case in point.[64] But if Woodberry too much admired what is bookish, Greenough White and later iconoclasts too much admire what is merely brash; and literary investigators during the last twenty-five years have on the whole tended away from the naïve acceptance of a simple parallelism between England and the United States and toward the wiser, shrewder, and subtler suggestions of Woodberry. His critical judgments are academic, but his historical perceptions are finer than those of Wendell or Richardson.

4

The revolt signalized in literary history by the appearance of the Macy volume had, then, both negative and positive phases. Negatively, it was part of that general rebellion against the nineteenth century which swept the country during the second and third decades of our time. And since Victorianism was an awkward term to apply to the United States, the rebellion attacked two related concepts: something called Puritanism, held to be a restrictive force in art and life; and something called the genteel tradition, which, it was thought, hugely overestimated writers like Longfellow and Lowell and underestimated (or failed to estimate at all) geniuses like Melville and Thoreau. Positively, the new movement sought to create literary history in its own image; that is, it deliberately tried to rewrite the story of American letters in values known only to the twentieth century. Every age, of course, remakes history in its own image, but the special mark of these iconoclasts was a refusal of historical importance as a canon of judgment. The international influence of Cooper, for example, is a function of his narrative power, but the new history, apologetic about the novelist, crowed with delight over Cooper the social critic. So, too, if Longfellow had been (next to Tennyson) the most beloved poet of the nineteenth century, the new history held that both the popularity and the poetry must per se be false, and made no effort to discover what it was in Longfellow that satisfied some deep spiritual need in his countrymen, and none to appraise him as an artist. Some critics—H. L. Mencken is an example—were political conservatives, but an assumption common to many was that the Jefferson tradition is more essentially "American" than is the tradition of Hamilton, so that political judgments sometimes replaced aesthetic criticism. Yet even this test was inconsistently applied. Critics rediscovered Freneau as a revolutionary, but scornfully set aside *Uncle Tom's Cabin,* even more portentous as a political manifestation, in favor of relatively forgotten works like Helper's *Impending Crisis.* They acclaimed Davy Crockett and forgot Mr. Dooley; praised the prose of Lincoln and deprecated the rhetoric of Webster, albeit the economic views of these two statesmen were not worlds apart; acclaimed Emily Dickinson, who had no political ideas; and ignored William Cullen Bryant, who had a great many of them. In general, the new movement differed sharply from the nineteenth-century critics in making American prose rather than American poetry the focus of its interest. Stedman, chief historian of verse in the nineteenth century, has not yet had an adequate successor, whereas the complaint of Professor C. Alphonso Smith in 1904 [65] that no history of the American novel had been written is now a mere historical curiosity. We shall return to certain aspects of this intellectual revolution.

The iconoclasts moved in three companies: Jeffersonians Marxists, and Freudians. The most widely influential history produced in the twenties was, of course, Parrington's *Main Currents in American Thought* (1927–1930) in three volumes (the last fragmentary), which does not, however, purport to be a history of American literature. Courses in American history found the work immensely useful because of its correlation of political event and literary document; and since professors of American literature, despairing of equitable treatment from English departments, were substituting a social and political frame of reference for the customary philological lore, Parrington seemed for a time almost to obliterate literary histories, even in the history of American literature. *Main Currents in American Thought* is probably the most brilliant publishing success in the whole range of our general topic.

The way for such a history had been long prepared, not merely by the growth of American sociology and the development of American economic interpretation, but also in the general fields of intellectual and literary history and criticism. As early as 1887, a reviewer of Richardson had said:

> We need to have discussed, in their direct bearings on our literature, the political situation for fifty years with reference to slavery, in its stages of compromise, agitation, and war; the religious situation about our literary metropolis, in its stages of revolt and triumph, as expressed in "Our Liberal Movement in Theology;" the social relations of class to class through the transitions from oneness to separation, cooperation, antagonism; the industrial situation, in the gradual transfer of life from country to city; the individual environment of our writers, wherein the division-of-labor principle has been inoperative; for our literary men have largely been workers as well as thinkers. . . . All these influences, and more, should have place in a critical history of American literature.[66]

Garland had declared in 1894 that "if you would raise the standard of art in America you must raise the standard of living"; [67] and Howells, in his brilliant analysis of "The Man of Letters as a Man of Business," included in *Literature and Life* (1902), had produced almost the only document one can profitably consult about the relation of author, publisher, and audience as a problem in economics. Others had lamented the neglect of the politician and the businessman by both writers and literary historians; [68] a symposium in the *Bookman* in 1914 had noted the relation between fiction and social and political unrest; [69] and a full-dress discussion of "The New Economic Interpretation of Literary History" by Elbridge Colby in 1913 had debated the pros and cons of the relation of imaginative art to national and commercial expansion.[70] Obviously, Parrington is not a mere economic determinist; the point is that a way was opening for his kind of history.[71]

The nature of Parrington's work is so widely known as to make discussion almost superfluous. That the book is blind to aesthetic charm and callous toward what I may call the total literary problem; that Parrington was hostile to New England Puritanism, much too generous to French philosophy, and far too unsympathetic in the case of the metaphysical speculation which did not have immediate utilitarian ends in view; that he conceived the Hamiltonian tradition as an enemy to be fought in that warfare between Ormuzd and Ahrimanes which was for him central in American existence; that he neglected or minimized vast irrational forces below the level of the mind—those energies which fascinated Ludwig Lewisohn and D. H. Lawrence—all this is true enough. Indeed, to go back to Parrington after studying Schneider's *History of American Philosophy,* Miller's *New England Mind,* and Ralph Barton Perry's *Puritanism and Democracy* is to find him metallic and thin. But who can forget the tingling sense of discovery with which we first read these lucid pages, followed this confident marshaling of masses of stubborn material into position, until book, chapter, and section became as orderly as a regiment on parade! Readers in 1927 felt the same quality of excitement, I imagine, as Jeffrey experienced

141

when in 1825 young Macaulay sent his dazzling essay on Milton to the *Edinburgh Review*. All other histories of literature were compelled to pale their intellectual fires. We were free of Anglophilism, of colonialism, of apology at last. The very title proclaimed our right to rival Georg Brandes' *Main Currents of Nineteenth Century Literature*. Here, for the first time, the intellectual life of the Old South became an intelligible program. Here, forgotten names— Daniel Leonard, Robert Treat Paine, W. J. Grayson—took on flesh and blood and played understandable roles in the drama of the national past. A phrase from the "Foreword" to *The Colonial Mind* characterizes the driving power of this work—"a conviction of the greatness of the issues and the intellectual honesty and masculine vigor of the disputants." Here was a usable past, adult, reasonable, coherent.

In *Main Currents in American Thought* two tendencies are fused. The brilliant individual characterizations, enriched by affirmative or damaging quotations, the seeking out of a *qualité maîtresse* in a writer, as when Parrington says of Samuel Sewall: "In his religious life he was the same prudent, plodding soul, that stowed away in his strongbox deeds to ample possessions during his pilgrimage"— these devices remind us that this historian is heir of a tradition stretching back through Moses Coit Tyler and Taine to Sainte-Beuve. But he is also a child of the eighteenth century, which was his spirit's home. His ideals are lucidity, order, a scrupulous and efficient prose. He builds as Gibbon or Voltaire built books—orderly paragraphs marching to schematized ideas. The table of contents to the unfinished third volume is a debater's outline, a lawyer's brief, and shows us how he worked, for his aim is not merely the right word in the right place but also the right author under the right subhead of an argument developed with mathematical rigor. Moreover, his theories of human nature likewise descend from the Enlightenment, or at least from utilitarianism. Because men are supposed to know and follow their best interests, the duty of the writer in America is to persuade and convince, to clarify, defend, and denounce, but not to charm, to astonish, to enrich the soul. The business of style is to achieve the utmost transparency, since that is the best way so to clothe one's logic that it will be understood of all people. Indeed, Parrington's notorious failures, as in the case of Poe, do not arise so much from his inability to appreciate poetry as from his inability to comprehend human beings who do not accept the eighteenth-century ideal of man. When life is a battle and a march, especially in the United States, no author has the right to dream, least of all a man of Poe's brain power.

One can imagine an intelligent conversation between Parrington, the twentieth-century liberal, and Dr. Johnson, the eighteenth-century Tory, because they would share certain tacit assumptions about man in society, but I cannot imagine a conversation between Parrington and Walter Pater, or between Parrington and Baudelaire, or between Parrington and Dostoevski. Our search for a usable past projected an eighteenth-century temperament into the world of Freud, Einstein, Kafka, and T. S. Eliot, surely an astonishing anachronism in a literary world that has gone all out for expressionism, sublimation, and the stream-of-consciousness novel!

"I was a good deal of a Marxian," Parrington wrote in 1928, though he came to doubt the sufficiency of the Marxian formula. No such doubt troubles the vigorous prose of V. F. Calverton, whose *Liberation of American Literature* (1932) is an impressive analysis of literary history in terms of the class struggle. To say, however, that class consciousness came in with Marxist criticism would be wrong. Not to speak of the conscious class distinctions involved in the *de haut en bas* attitude of the "dominant" cultural class toward powerful, uneducated democracy in the early years of the Republic, a conservative group, painfully conscious of its dwindling authority, thrust class distinctions upon the literary scene long before World War I, notably soon after the effects of the "New Immigration" began to be felt. The American lecture tour of Matthew Arnold dramatized the problem of aristocracy confronting cultural *hoi polloi;* [72] and there is some reason to interpret the whole Anglophile tradition in the schools and colleges as a measure for cultural control on the part of "Old Americans" over lesser breeds without the law. Barrett Wendell, in volumes entitled *Liberty, Union and Democracy* (1906) and *The Privileged Classes* (1908), made explicit what was implicit in his *Literary History;* namely, his belief that a governing class of "Old Americans," the wise and good, should rule: "Among the commonplaces of our century and more of republican eloquence you will find innumerable thoughtless assertions of human equality which, if duly reasoned out by any process of ordinary logic, would start us along toward anarchy." He advocated a union of laissez-faire economics, education, and culture, which led him to observe: "If it be true . . . that, having rid the world of avowed privilege in favour of the responsible, we are unwittingly shackling it again with unperceived privilege in favour of the irresponsible," we have abandoned the original Calvinist (and

144

New England) belief that the wise and good (and wealthy) should be forever favored.[73] Nor was Wendell's a solitary voice. In 1915 H. St. George Tucker, Katherine Fullerton Gerould, and C. H. A. Wager lifted voices in favor of what can only be called an aristocratic theory of literature ("Culture," wrote Mrs. Gerould, "has ceased to be a passionate American preoccupation"); in 1916 H. Houston Peckham, Agnes Repplier, Robert Underwood Johnson, and G. R. Elliott in varying degrees mourned for a literary past controlled by the wise and good; [74] and of course the entire Humanist group, despite protestations of republican virtue, argued in fact for reverting to a culture controlled by an aristocratic few. The new writers of the twenties, said Paul Elmer More, are "quite innocent of education in any such sense as would be recognized in Paris or London"; Sinclair Lewis was, he thought, intellectually crude; and, like his compeers, More demanded that writers return to the "discipline of sound humanism, which will train the imagination in loyalty to the great traditions, while cherishing the liberty to think and the power to create without succumbing to the seductions of the market place or the gutter." [75] The *words* involved no class consciousness; the fact, however, pleaded for the supremacy of the wise and good. Marxian critics did not invent class feeling in the 1930's.

Since the occupational disease of American literary histories, however ostentatious their prefaces, has been to have no point of view at all, the Calverton history has the considerable merit of maintaining a point of view throughout its five-hundred pages. The difficulty is that all is fish that comes to the Marxian net—the frontier, American magazines, the novels of Dreiser, Calvinism, the Old South, the populist movement, the loneliness of Nathaniel Hawthorne. A book which proclaims that Mark Twain is "the first American prose writer of any importance," which says of Edgar Allan Poe, who seems never to have read German, that "he turned to Germany instead of to England for his inspiration," which, lavishing space upon Jack London, fails to record the effect of wealth upon his later books, and which, dismissing the *Atlantic Monthly* in a sentence or two, devotes ten pages to the *Masses*, the *Liberator*, and the *New Masses*, is not, at any rate, dull. It is, however, easy to be put off by slips of fact and eccentricities of statement. The noble plea with which the volume ends—a plea for "a return of that faith in the common man, in the mass, but a faith founded upon a collective instead of an individualistic premise" [76]—raises again the vexed question with which the history of American literary history begins; namely, the nature of the relation between literary art and the society for which the art is produced.

Madame de Staël had thought that republican institutions must necessarily produce republican literature. Calverton and the Marxists desire a similar interplay between communist literature and the communist state; or, failing that, they wish to enlist literature on the side of revolution. Writes Joseph Freeman: "The vast, creative experiences of the revolutionary workers and their intellectual allies must of necessity produce a new art, an art that will take over the best in the old culture and add to it new insights, new methods, new forms appropriate for the experience of our epoch." [77] To deny that good writing has sprung from this premise would be idle, just as it would be idle to deny that, belligerent though Marxian literary criticism is, it sometimes has values of vigor and insight.[78] But as a basis of literary history the axiom that class consciousness is central seems incredibly naïve; nor does the translation of Plekhanov's *Art and Society* (1936) [79] give us a very persuasive document, inasmuch as it is by no means a profound discovery that French drama and painting in the eighteenth century reflect the conflict of aristocratic and bourgeois values—an observation one does not have to be a Marxist critic to make. On the other hand, it is idle to remark that the error of Marxist theorizing is to pin its faith to the one basic element that any writer (who cannot change his sex or his race) can alter, namely, his class; and Calverton is not so simple-minded as to argue that the values of the bourgeoisie are immediately reflected in American books of value.

To disentangle fact from theory in Calverton's pages, to sort out what is valuable in his analysis from the merely tendentious would require a long series of demonstrations; and I shall so far indulge the vanity of dogmatizing as to say that literary history is an intricate problem, social analysis a problem even more intricate, and the historical relation between these two constellations of difficulties is, if these pages have any meaning, more difficult still. Thus far, no American historian in the Marxist camp has succeeded in mastering all these masses of detail and generalizing from them. What Marxian interpretation has done, it seems to me, notably in the instances of V. F. Calverton, Granville Hicks, and Bernard Smith,[80] has been to compel the academic historian to remember that the bibliographical and aesthetic worlds are set in universes of economic and social discourse, to remember that taste is not a private matter but a public charge, and, particularly in the American field, to include in literary history much

147

that was once regarded as beneath the dignity of scholar-ship.

The immense vogue of Freud in America [81] made it in-evitable that the psychology of the subconscious and of the unconscious, whether Freudian or otherwise, should be-come an instrument for analyzing cultural and literary his-tory. The way was paved by Waldo Frank, Van Wyck Brooks, and D. H. Lawrence [82] for the most considerable book of this order. If Calverton sought to trace the libera-tion of literature from the tyranny of middle-class economic interest, in *Expression in America* (1932), Ludwig Lewi-sohn attempted to demonstrate the necessity of freeing it from repressions engendered by "Puritanism" and the tyranny of the genteel. He remarks that the "only artist tolerated" in the American past has been "the artificer who observed the rules of the social and moral game." He held that "any attempt to speak out was felt during the greater part of the American past to be a danger and a betrayal." In the endeavor to speak out, Lewisohn set himself the task of writing two books at once. One is a critical survey of the national letters; the second is a volume which alternates between the psychology of Freud and the economic de-terminism of Charles A. Beard. The thesis that is supposed to bind the two together is a doctrine of the personality of the artist:

This total man, this artist who is impelled to publish himself to his fellows is impelled to do so because he belongs to them and they to him; he is part of the collectivity even as rebel and revolutionary; he is mouthpiece first of his clan and race and city, next of all mankind, because he is integral part of race and clan and kind.

148

As in the case of Calverton, so in the case of Lewisohn, one has to get around or forget many errors of fact and numerous eccentric judgments. We read that Emerson and Thoreau were "chilled under-sexed valetudinarians," that Poe sustained a trauma in infancy, that Whitman was a homosexual of a "most pronounced and aggressive type," that the novels of Howells are "acutely and negatively sex-conscious"; [83] but when we ask how and why Mr. Lewisohn is sure of these things, there is no answer, for there is no objective evidence. Since psychoanalysis depends upon the uncovering of submerged memories through free association under skillful guidance, it seems fair to remark that a dead author has neither memories nor associations nor the capacity to be cross-examined; and though his literary remains may contain overt or hidden symbolism of considerable psychic significance, the interpretation of these symbols varies so greatly from practitioner to practitioner as to reduce control of the material to zero. Literary interpretation and literary history thus become anybody's game.

The virtue of Mr. Lewisohn's book was to place emphasis upon the Dionysiac aspect of art. The American record may have been in this regard Alexandrian; it has scarcely been Apollonian. Lewisohn insisted that any art is the expression—indeed, the explosion—of energy, not merely a problem in morals or a segment of the history of ideas. The writers he best analyzes are energetic men like Whitman and Mark Twain. He sees a kind of fury at work in American life, which he wants both expressed and sublimated in literary expression worthy of our primary powers; and if genteel historians had called upon American bards to imitate Tennyson and read Arnold, Lewisohn now directs them to sit at the feet of Goethe or of Nietzsche. The wheel comes full circle in *Expression in America,* for the argument that American literature should be shaggy, powerful, and unique is here re-enforced by the command to come out of the America of Longfellow and Howells and to take example, if necessary, from powerful foreigners unafraid of sex and vitality. To glance back in thought up the long road we have come, to remember that the American muse was originally adjured to be a Christian, and then to read in Lewisohn that the Christian tradition in American culture has been a principal barrier to a free and fearless national literature is to realize how, even in the staid world of literary history, the whirligig of time brings in his revenges.

## NOTES TO CHAPTER V

[1] John Macy, *The Critical Game* (New York, 1922), p. 216.

[2] Macy, *The Spirit of American Literature* (Modern Library ed.; New York, 1913), pp. vii, 12, 13, vi. He dismissed Edwards as a "dreadful bore" (p. vi).

[3] *Hawthorne* ("English Men of Letters"; New York, 1879), pp. 12, 44, 3. James enumerated the "items of high civilization" absent from American life: "No State, in the European sense of the word, and indeed barely a specific national name. No sovereign, no court, no personal loyalty, no aristocracy, no church, no clergy, no army, no diplomatic service, no country gentlemen, no palaces, no castles, nor manors, nor old country-houses, nor parsonages, nor thatched cottages, nor ivied ruins; no cathedrals, nor abbeys, nor little Norman churches; no great Universities nor public schools—no Oxford, nor Eton, nor Harrow; no literature, no novels, no museums, no pictures, no political society, no sporting class—no Epsom nor Ascot!" But he can be taken too literally; as he said, "The American knows that a good deal remains" (pp. 42–43).

[4] Kinahan Cornwallis, "American Literature and Authorship," *Manhattan,* II(3), 270 (September, 1883).

[5] Charles Eliot Norton, "The Intellectual Life of America," *New Princeton Review,* VI (n.s. 3), 312–324 (November, 1888).

[6] Henry C. Vedder, *American Writers of To-day* (New York, 1894), pp. vi, 3, 4.

[7] Hamilton Wright Mabie, "American Literature and American Nationality," *Forum,* XXVI(5), 634 (January, 1899).

[8] Oscar Lovell Triggs, "A Century of American Poetry," *Forum,* XXX(5), 640 (January, 1901). This is a thoughtful review.

[9] These gems are from Charles A. Conant, "The Literature of Expansion," *International,* III, 720 (June, 1901), the article being an argument that literary men should be "at the same time practical"; "Editor's Easy Chair," *Harper's Monthly Magazine,* CV(629), 803 (October, 1902), an essay which finds the state of American letters "deplorable" precisely at a time when the English seem more friendly; Francis Lamont Pierce, "A Survey of Contemporary American Literature," *Arena,* XXXVIII(217), 622 (December, 1907)— reprinted in part, in *Current Literature,* XLIV(4), 387–388 (April, 1908); George F. Parker, "Some American Literary Needs," *Sewanee Review,* XVIII(1), 3 (January, 1910); Edwin Björkman, "An Open Letter to President Wilson on Behalf of American Literature," *Century,* LXXXVII(6), 888 (April, 1914).

[10] James H. Collins, "Literary Methods," *Bookman,* XXIII(4), 443–447 (June, 1906).

[11] Charles Leonard Moore, "The Interregnum in American Literature," *Dial,* XLVIII(573), 307–309 (May 1, 1910).

[12] Hanna Astrup Larsen, "The Cowardice of American Literature," *Forum,* XLVIII(4), 445, 449 (October, 1912). In *World Today,* XIII(4), 1012–1016 (October, 1907) John Rothwell Slater dismissed American literary criticism as "nauseatingly fulsome"; and in *Their Day in Court* Percival Pollard got rid of American literature as both crowded and worthless. See *Current Literature,* XLVII(6), 630–633 (December, 1909).

[13] Walt Whitman, "Poetry of the Future," *North American Review,* CXXXII(291), 195–210 (February, 1881), reprinted as "Poetry To-day in America," in *Specimen Days;* and "Have We a National Literature?" *North American Review,* CLII(412), 332–338 (March, 1891).

[14] James Herbert Morse, "The Native Element in American Fiction," *Century,* XXVI(2), 288–298 (June, 1883); *ibid.,* XXVI(3),

362–375 (July, 1883). This is an able history of American novelists.

[15] Julian Hawthorne, "The American Element in Fiction," *North American Review*, CXXXIX(333), 168 (August, 1884).

[16] W. Balestier, "Recent American Fiction," *Church Review*, XLVII(160), 272–285 (January, 1886).

[17] Hamlin Garland, "Productive Conditions of American Literature," *Forum*, XVII(6), 698 (August, 1894).

[18] B. W. Wells, "Contemporary American Essayists," *Forum*, XXIII(4), 496 (June, 1897).

[19] William P. Trent, "American Literature," *Dial*, XXVIII(333), 334–340 (May 1, 1900). This article repays careful reading.

[20] See, among other things, "Editor's Study," *Harper's*, CVII(640), 646–648 (September, 1903); W. D. Howells, "A Hundred Years of American Verse," *North American Review*, CLXXII(1), 148–160 (January, 1901), where the phrase occurs; and Howells, "Literary Recollections," *North American Review*, CXCV(4), 550–558 (April, 1912).

[21] Winifred Webb, "The Spirit of American Literature," *Arena*, XXXVI(200), 121–125 (August, 1906). The line of Mrs. Atherton's comments may be gleaned from a succession of articles and interviews. See *Bookman*, XIV(2), 137–138 (October, 1901); *Bookman*, XVII(1), 36–37 (March, 1903); *Current Literature*, XLIV(2), 158–160 (February, 1908); *Bookman*, XXX(6), 633–640 (February, 1910).

[22] See chap. 3.

[23] *Independent*, LIV(2816), 2784–2786 (November 20, 1902). See also Grace I. Colbron, "The Reading Zones of the United States," *Bookman*, XXXVI(2), 148–152 (October, 1912).

[24] Hamlin Garland, "The West in Literature," *Arena*, VI(6), 669 (November, 1892). See also the comment in the *Review of Reviews*, VIII(46), 569 (November, 1893) on Garland's "Literary Emancipation of the West."

[25] Frank Norris, "A Neglected Epic," *World's Work*, V, 2905, 2906 (December, 1902). See also an article in the *Dial* for November, 1893, on the same theme; the article is summarized in the *Review of Reviews*, VIII(46), 568 (November, 1893). And see Arthur Chapman, "The New West and the Old Fiction," *Independent*, LIV(2771), 98–100 (January 9, 1902).

[26] Herbert Bashford, "The Literary Development of the Far Northwest," *Overland Monthly*, XXXIII, 316–320 (April, 1899).

[27] Bashford, "The Literary Development of the Pacific Coast,"

*Atlantic Monthly,* XCII(549), 4 (July, 1903). Cf. this passage:
"To what extent the splendor and majesty of the West may favor the
growth of a peculiarly distinctive literature is altogether speculative,
but if we are to be guided in our forecast by the history of other
lands, we may assume with some degree of certainty that this beauty
and sublimity of landscape will ultimately make itself manifest in a
greater breadth of canvas, a bolder stroke, and in the more varied
and brilliant coloring of a lavish brush. . . . The tendency of California writers is toward ruggedness and strength, . . . not . . . a
weak imitation of those mouldy, yet revered models of antiquity
known as the classics" (p. 8). This is, of course, the restatement of a
theme from colonial times.

[28] George Edward Woodberry, "The South in American Letters,"
*Harper's,* CVII(641), 735–741 (October, 1903).

[29] Benjamin W. Wells, "Southern Literature of the Year," *Forum,*
XXIX(4), 501–512 (June, 1900).

[30] The original edition of the *Library of Southern Literature* was
in fifteen volumes, published simultaneously in New Orleans, At-
lanta, and Dallas; a sixteenth is variously copyrighted as 1907, 1910,
and 1913; and a seventeenth appeared in 1923. There was an
impressive editorial board headed by E. A. Alderman and Joel Chan-
dler Harris, but the work wavered between scholarly objectivity and
local pride. In the *Sewanee Review* for April, 1907, Henry N. Snyder
has an interesting article called "The Matter of 'Southern Literature'" in which he analyzes the theory of a literary history of the
South, the article being apparently occasioned by the appearance of
the anthology.

[31] See Hamilton Wright Mabie, "The Poetry of the South," *International,* V(2), 200–223 (February, 1902), in which he contrasts
northern and southern bards by assuming that New England stood
still.

[32] See the definitive article by Herbert R. Brown, "The Great
American Novel," *American Literature,* VII(1), 1–14 (March,
1935), together with its rich supporting bibliography.

[33] H. W. Boynton, "A Glance at Current American Fiction," *Nation,* LXXXVIII(2275), 106 (February 4, 1909).

[34] Realism in American fiction during the eighties, thought Margaret Anderson, chose not the commonplace, but the heroic, great,
and tragic elements (*Dial,* XXIII(274), 269–270, November 16,
1897); and in 1901 Henry A. Beers argued that the Civil War wound
up one literary era and opened another, the spirit of the new age

being "observant, social, dramatic," its expression "the novel of real life, the short story, the dialect sketch." See "Literature and the Civil War," *Atlantic,* LXXXVIII(530), 749–760 (December, 1901). As for the historical novel, Paul Leicester Ford argued it was a corrective of the "Afternoon Tea Novel," which he heartily despised ("The American Historical Novel," *Atlantic,* LXXX(482), 721–728, December, 1897); and by 1902 Annie Russell Marble believed that historical fiction had attained sure rank in contemporary American literature and represented a healthy reaction against morbid realism and elementary local tales. Furthermore, these novels were essentially "American"; they showed the "true man, stripped of his insignia" (*Dial,* XXXII(383), 369–372, June 1, 1902).

[35] H. H. Boyeson, "Why We Have No Great Novelists," *Forum,* II(6), 615–622 (February, 1887); M. H. Lawless, "The American Novel," *The Author,* II(5), 63–64 (May 15, 1890); Ezra S. Brudno, "The American Novel," *Bookman,* XIX(4), 414–417 (June, 1904); Louise Collier Willcox, "The Content of the Modern Novel," *North American Review,* CLXXXII(6), 919–929 (June, 1906); Frederick Taber Cooper, "The Social Structure and Some Recent Novels," *Bookman,* XXXVI(1), 64–71 (September, 1912); "American and English Novelists," *Nation,* XCVIII(2546), 422–423 (April 16, 1914); Edward Garnett, "Some Remarks on American and English Fiction," *Atlantic,* CXIV(6), 747–756 (December, 1914).

[36] Robert Herrick, "The Background of the American Novel," *Yale Review,* III (2), 213–233 (January, 1914). For interesting comment see the editorial in the *Dial,* LVI(661), 5–7 (January 1, 1914).

[37] Hamilton Wright Mabie, *Books and Culture* (New York, 1896), pp. 72, 253, 265.

[38] "The Future of American Letters," *American,* I(20), 323 (February 26, 1881).

[39] Richard Watson Gilder, "Certain Tendencies in Current Literature," *New Princeton Review,* n.s. IV(1), 1–13 (July, 1887).

[40] "A Century of American Verse," *Dial,* XXIX, 258 (October 16, 1900).

[41] "Americanism in Literature," *Outlook,* LXXII(14), 772–774 (December 6, 1902), p. 773.

[42] Benjamin A. Heydrick, "Poetry," *Chautauquan,* LXV(2), 187–188 (January, 1912).

[43] Robert Underwood Johnson, "The Responsibilities of the Magazine," *Independent,* LXXIII(3343), 1489 (December 26, 1912).

[44] Archibald Henderson, "Democracy and Literature," *South Atlantic Quarterly*, XII(2), 97, 98 (April, 1913).

[45] See the review by Carl Becker in the *Dial*, LVI, 140–142.

[46] See, in addition, Will D. Howe, "American Literature," *Reader Magazine*, IV(5), 589–595, 715–720 (Oct.–Nov., 1904); Carl Holliday, "The Philosophy of American Poetry," *Sewanee Review*, XIII(1), 86–101 (January, 1905); Walter Hines Page, "The Writer and the University," *Atlantic*, C(5), 685–695 (November, 1907); Florence E. Hyde, "A Plea for Nobler Ideals in American Literature," *Education*, XXX(8), 481–493 (April, 1910); "The Ethical Dominant in American Poetry," *Current Literature*, LI(3), 323–326 (September, 1911); and almost any of the textbook histories of literature. Even Guglielmo Ferrero, writing on "The Riddle of America" in the *Atlantic*, CXII(5), 702–713 (November, 1913), found that pragmatism, far from illustrating American materialism, was but an aspect of idealism.

[47] "American Poetry," *American*, I(16), 250 (January 29, 1881).

[48] "Wanted—An American Novel," Boston *Literary World*, XIV, 192 (June 16, 1883). But see the reply on August 11, p. 259.

[49] H. Pancoast, "The Intellectual Life of America," *Andover Review*, XI(1), 166 (February, 1889). This is in part a reply to Charles Eliot Norton and in part an attack on commercialism.

[50] This seems to be the inference to be drawn from Charles Leonard Moore, "Tendencies of American Literature in the Closing Quarter of the Century," *Dial*, XXIX(345), 295–297 (November 1, 1900). See also E. Cavazza, "A Bird's-Eye View of American Literature," *Unitarian Review*, XXXV(4), 295–304 (April, 1891); Charles Johnston, "The True American Spirit in Literature," *Atlantic*, LXXXIV(51), 29–35 (July, 1899); "Richard Whiteing on American Fiction," *Bookman*, XVI(5), 444–445 (January, 1903); Charles Whibley, "American Literature," *Living Age*, CCLVII(3328), 137–143 (April 18, 1908).

[51] T. Watts, "The Future of American Literature," *Eclectic Magazine*, LIV(n.s. 1), 94 (July, 1891). The circulation by reprint or otherwise of British comment on American literature is an element in the problem.

[52] "Three Centuries of American Literature," *Dial*, XXIX(348), 485–487 (December 16, 1900). See also William Morton Payne's review in the *Atlantic*, LXXXVII(521), 411–418 (March, 1901).

[53] Brander Matthews, "An American Critic on American Literature," *Forum*, XLIII(1), 81 (January, 1910).

[54] See the article entitled "To Cool Our Literary Pride," *Literary Digest*, XLVIII(8), 380 (February 21, 1914). H. Houston Peckham, "Is American Literature Read and Respected in Europe?" *South Atlantic Quarterly*, XIII(4), 382 (October, 1914); John Laurence McMaster, "The American Pegasus" (July), pp. 213–219.

[55] William Cranston Lawton, "Classical Influences upon American Literature," *Chautauquan*, XXX, 466–470 (February, 1900).

[56] Henry James, *Partial Portraits* (1888), pp. 7, 21.

[57] See the interesting review in the *Overland Monthly*, n.s. XIV, 549–556 (1889).

[58] Katharine Lee Bates, *American Literature* (New York, 1898), pp. 128, 131.

[59] Edwin Percy Whipple, *American Literature and Other Papers* (Boston, 1896), especially pp. 1–61. The essay degenerates into a catalogue.

[60] Fred Lewis Pattee, *A History of American Literature with a View to the Fundamental Principles Underlying Its Development* (New York, 1896), especially pp. iv, 1–4. Pattee was to do better work.

[61] William P. Trent, *A History of American Literature, 1607–1865* (New York, 1903), p. 11. Though Trent argues that American literature is "a creation of the nineteenth century," his refusal to deal with living writers truncated his study.

[62] Brownell sought no general law governing the development of American prose, but in a striking article in the *Atlantic*, LXXXVII (523), 689–696 (May, 1901) entitled "American Prose Style," J. D. Logan, passing from the assumption that "the state of American society from its very beginning was eminently such as to express itself in a passion for deeds," and observing that our writers are characteristically "citizen authors" writing a "citizen literature," found the special quality of American prose to be manliness—that is, its goal is immediate, common, and of vivid interest amongst men of fine good sense. What he was trying to do, I think, was to formulate some clear statement of the more rapid rhythm and nervous tension of American English.

[63] Greenough White, *The Philosophy of American Literature* (Boston, 1890), especially pp. iv, iii, 12–14, 15, 46–47, 49–50.

[64] George E. Woodberry, *America in Literature* (New York, 1903), especially pp. 191, 211, 218. Some of Woodberry's essay chapters had earlier appeared in the magazines.

[65] C. Alphonso Smith, "The Novel in America," *Sewanee Review,* XII(2), 158–166 (April, 1904).

[66] J. J. Halsey, "American Literature," *Dial,* VII(82), 245 (February, 1887).

[67] Hamlin Garland, "The Land Question and Its Relation to Art and Literature," *Arena,* IX(50), 166 (January, 1894).

[68] Arthur Bartlett Maurice, "The Politician as Literary Material," *Bookman,* XI(2), 120–121 (April, 1900); William Arthur Gill, "Some Novelists and the Business Man," *Atlantic,* CXII(3), 374–385. (September, 1913); *ibid.,* CXII(4), 506–515 (October, 1913). This is a comparison of the treatment of the theme in British and American fiction.

[69] *Bookman,* XL(3), 276–303 (November, 1914). Contributors included Sinclair Lewis, whose theme is that novelists cannot escape public questions.

[70] Elbridge Colby, "The New Economic Interpretation of Literary History," *South Atlantic Quarterly,* XII(4), 347–355 (October, 1913). Colby takes off, as it were, from Brander Matthews' discussion in *Gateways to Literature.*

[71] Parrington's discussion of the relation between Darwinism and American critical thought is partially anticipated in William Morton Payne's "American Literary Criticism and the Doctrine of Evolution," *International,* II(1), 26–46 (July, 1900); *ibid.,* II(2), 127–153 (August, 1900). Payne tends to equate acceptance of evolutionary thought and the "scientific spirit," and to argue that "the history of literature is the history of a process, and the study of a work of literature is the study of a product."

[72] On the curious fusion of racism, cultural snobbery, wealth, and honest concern for "culture" involved in Arnold's tour, see my article, "Arnold, Aristocracy, and America," *American Historical Review,* XLIX(3), 393–409 (April, 1944).

[73] Barrett Wendell, *Liberty, Union and Democracy: The National Ideals of America* (New York, 1906), p. 64; *The Privileged Classes* (New York, 1908), p. 51.

[74] H. St. George Tucker, "What Is Wrong with American Literature?" *South Atlantic Quarterly,* XIV(1), 47–52 (January, 1915); Katherine Fullerton Gerould, "The Extirpation of Culture," *Atlantic,* CXVI(4), 445–455 (October, 1915); Charles H. A. Wager, "Democracy and Literature," *ibid.,* pp. 479–486 (in a thorough-going democracy literature must become an anachronism[!]); H. Houston Peckham, "Lopsided Realism," *South Atlantic Quarterly,* XV(3),

276–281 (July, 1916); Agnes Repplier, "Americanism," *Atlantic*, CXVII(3), 289–297 (March, 1916); *Independent*, LXXXVIII (3545), 277 (November 13, 1916)—statement of Robert Underwood Johnson in defense of the American Academy and National Institute of Arts and Letters; G. R. Elliott, "New Poetry and New America," *Nation*, CVII(2787), 652–654 (November 30, 1918). These are merely representative of a larger group.

[75] Paul Elmer More, "Modern Current in American Literature," *Forum*, LXXIX(1), 136 (January, 1928).

[76] V. F. Calverton, *The Liberation of American Literature* (New York, 1932), p. 480.

[77] *Proletarian Literature in the United States: An Anthology*, ed. Joseph Freeman (New York, 1935), "Introduction," p. 19.

[78] There are representative selections in *Proletarian Literature in the United States*.

[79] George V. Plekhanov, *Art and Society*, translated from the Russian, with an introduction by Granville Hicks (New York, 1936). Besides the extended essay noted in the text on eighteenth-century France, this volume contains a second essay demonstrating that "the cry of art for art's sake was a great hoax on the bourgeoisie." According to the translator, Plekhanov "reaches the heart of the matter with one incision" in two paragraphs the reader will find on p. 56. I confess, after the third reading, I am no wiser.

[80] Granville Hicks, *The Great Tradition* (New York, 1933), which should, however, be read in the revised edition of 1935; and Bernard Smith, *Forces in American Criticism* (New York, 1939).

[81] F. J. Hoffman, *Freudianism and the Literary Mind* (Baton Rouge, 1945), is a satisfactory survey of the literary prestige and influence of Freud in the United States.

[82] Waldo Frank, *Our America* (New York, 1919); Van Wyck Brooks, *The Ordeal of Mark Twain* (New York, 1920); D. H. Lawrence, *Studies in Classic American Literature* (New York, 1923); Van Wyck Brooks, *The Pilgrimage of Henry James* (New York, 1925); Waldo Frank, *The Re-discovery of America* (New York, 1929). The influence of Freud upon this group of writers has not been uniform; and it should be said that Frazer's *Golden Bough* and a vague, popular anthropology has been important in their writings. Frank has been the chief interpreter of modern American writing to Latin America, notably Argentina.

[83] Ludwig Lewisohn, *Expression in America* (New York, 1932), especially the introduction, pp. ix–xxxii, which establishes the theory.

My quotations about particular authors can be readily found by using the index. A later edition is retitled *The Story of American Literature* (1937). Two articles by Lewisohn are especially illuminating: "Tradition and Freedom," *Nation*, CXI(2892), 651–652 (December 8, 1920), and "America in Europe," *Saturday Review of Literature*, I(41), 737–738 (May 9, 1925).

# VI

# "On Native Grounds"

OF THE FOUR AUTHORS discussed in the previous chapter—Macy, Parrington, Calverton, and Lewisohn—only one was a professor of English, and his *Main Currents* is an exercise in social and political thought rather than in belles-lettres. It is now time to inquire what professional literary scholars have attempted in the twentieth century.

Universities are conservative, the humanities are among their more conservative divisions, and the learned societies humanists create are more conservative still. Nevertheless, when the Modern Language Association of America was founded in 1883 it was considered to be a young and radical organization struggling to wrest control of humanistic learning from the classicists—struggling to complete, in sum, what the Connecticut Wits had desiderated in the eighteenth century. As we have seen, the climate of opinion which shaped that organization was unfavorable to the scholarly study of American literature, and the triumph of the English departments checked American studies. In some sixty volumes of the *Publications of the Modern Language Association,* a paper by A. H. Smyth in 1887 is the sole evidence of professional responsibility for the national literature; and of the sixty-odd presidents of this association none has been distinguished for work in the American field. Moreover, the number of articles on American literary subjects in its publications is infinitesimal. When in a famous address of 1920 Professor John Matthews Manly proposed and secured the reorganization of this body to further its research interests, he ignored American literature; the committee which shaped the reorganization included no scholar in the field; and the forty-one groups into which the association was then subdivided did not recognize the subject by title—until 1930 research in American literary history appeared at the annual meeting disguised as "English XI" or "English XII."

Equal conservatism reigned in the universities. William B. Cairns at the University of Wisconsin seems to have been the sole professor of American literature in the country until 1917, when Fred Lewis Pattee was granted a similar title at Pennsylvania State College, thus increasing by 100 per cent the number of chairs specifically devoted to the national letters. Almost no college, however, lacked one or more professors of American history. Books by professors continued to be conservative vis-à-vis the problem of literary autonomy. In the twenties the rift between academic conservatism and American writing was deepened by the outpourings of the humanists—Babbitt, More, Sherman, Shafer, and others—who not only demanded that colleges concentrate upon European geniuses long dead, but also expressed a militant hostility to most American writing past and present. It was, according to their doctrines, infected with romanticism or with "naturism" or with both.[1] Even in the case of Professor Norman Foerster, one of the pioneers in furthering scholarly study in the American field, doctrine compelled him, in his *American Criticism*

(1928), to stretch critics upon the procrustean bed of theory and led him in an article of 1930 to cast doubt upon the validity of literary history itself.[2] And as late as the 1940's, surveys indicated a curious hesitation on the part of academic English departments to offer adequate instruction in American literature.[3]

Nevertheless, there was progress. In 1915 Pattee published his *History of American Literature Since 1870,* a significant pioneer work, outstripping in grasp and maturity his earlier "textbook" volume. Not only did it assume the existence of an autonomous literature, it also implied there was so much of it that a whole book could be devoted to less than half a century of development. Moreover, Pattee did not refer apologetically to the superiority of British genius; and in place of the random list of names which had hitherto passed for recent history he seriously discussed movements like local color, and devoted to writers like Mark Twain an amount of space equal to what in other books was consecrated to Thackeray or Pope. The same year saw the appearance of two other volumes portentous for the future—a translation of Leon Kellner's *Amerikanische Literatur,* a treatise which flatly denied that Americans have been too busy conquering a continent to produce a literature; and Woodbridge Riley's philosophical history, *American Thought from Puritanism to Pragmatism.* Kellner's assumption was that on which subsequent development was to build; and Riley's book, though it was not the first work on American philosophy, was the first orderly survey and may be said, if not to have invented, at any rate to have discovered a whole new field—that of the history of ideas in the United States.[4]

Among other causes which seem to have altered the climate of opinion about American literature was a curious renewal of the ancient quarrel about the relative merits of British and American literature, a discussion which occupied considerable space in the magazines between 1915 (or earlier) and the middle twenties. Waspish things were said on both sides. The novelist Meredith Nicholson, in response to earlier essays by Garnett and Canby, held that "the taste of many an American has been debased by English fiction" and called for a new Walt Whitman to emit a barbaric yawp in prose; and if that did not help—the article is confused—let literature acquire "real dignity as a profession." [5] That same year (1915) James Bryce hoped that British and American literatures were drawing closer together, but James Stephens, in an article in the *Century*, managed to annoy a good many readers by declaring that American authors had not yet learned how to write, asking what had happened to the promise of fifty years ago, and darkly advising the Americans to get rid of "the old woman as speedily as they can, and . . . put the boy back to discipline for a few years more." [6] Then followed a warm exchange of opinions, some designed to continue controversy, some intended as ironic. Characteristic comments are these:

> Our short stories are, in the mass, worlds beyond theirs [the British], because the American author, if he has less leisure, has a less narrow experience of life, draws his material from a more diversified *milieu*, and expresses himself less traditionally. . . .

> [The American literary schooner] scudding before the wind, with everything taut and ship-shape, [the British literary houseboat] drifting lazily down stream, with awnings and easy-chairs and hammocks and flower-boxes filling its decks . . .

163

But American critics, in their aim of hailing and supporting a native American literature, must make a continuous and sustained effort to penetrate the blank, rolling mist of conventional valuations.

If in the past our literature has been inherently English, and if at present it is partially English and partially Continental, there is no reason why in the future it may not be emphatically American.

The effect [of the clamor for Anglo-American co-operation] is largely to keep our authors from being original by making them strive after originality and to keep them from being truly and convincingly American by interfering with their being unconsciously themselves.

Maliciously, but with more than a grain of truth, one Harvard professor wrote of this tendency to look abroad for faults as good proof that New England and old England were, after all, at heart a nation one and indivisible.

The fact that much of the exceedingly sentimental American fiction and drama and poetry is very popular in England surely proves that we [British] have, in proportion to our population as many of the sloppy-minded in our midst as America has. . . .

English literature with its attitude toward class, with its comparative freedom from thought of money, has nothing in common with the pioneer literature of America.

We do not insist on Buffalo-Billism in pen and ink; but are we [British] wrong in hoping for something that will suggest America first and not France, . . . something that, however cultured or cultivated, is yet not exotic? [7]

These random passages, because they are picked at random, illustrate better than any formal analysis the intellectual vacuity of the dispute, which reminds one of the similar dispute a hundred years earlier. For example, answering Stephens' charge that American writers could not

164

produce good English, Harvey O'Higgins said of one of Stephens' own sentences that it represented disgraceful syntax.[8] Whereas Gilbert Cannan and John Middleton Murry somewhat futilely sought to find points of contact between young writers on both sides of the water,[9] John Gould Fletcher observed: "More than one American scholar may fairly be taken to represent that well-known anomaly the American student of poetry; who is so saturated with the alien music of English singers as to suppose you have only to sing in the same style to produce a masterpiece."[10] War psychology undoubtedly increased national self-consciousness, so much so that British observers like W. L. George, S. K. Ratcliffe, and Virginia Woolf were puzzled by it, just as they were puzzled by the violence of anti-British sentiment. Mrs. Woolf, in fact, concluded that the "English tradition" was now unable to cope with this vast land,[11] and the growing sense of cultural alienation may help to explain why, at long last, a British scholar at University College, London, in 1931 finally turned his attention to the problem of Anglo-American literary relations.[12]

Whether or not the guess be correct that this silly quarrel—further proof that the two countries were separated by a common language—shook the faith of English departments in the superiority of British letters; whether a war-created nationalism helped to swing the balance; whether Professor Boynton was correct in 1918 when he insisted that teachers should teach that "in American literature [there are] a fine constant of national magnanimity, and a broadening consciousness of a national debt";[13] or whether a new attitude resulted from what Paul Reinsch called "the inner freedom of American intellectual life,"[14] certain it is that the higher study of American literature turned the corner after World War I. For the first time in American history, professors of the subject pooled their resources in two works, published some seven years apart. These were the *Cambridge History of American Literature,* in four volumes (or rather, in three volumes, one of which was split in two), published from 1917 to 1921; and *A Reinterpretation of American Literature,* a collection of nine essays on theory and method, together with useful bibliographies, the whole edited by Norman Foerster in 1928. The first of these titles looked backward; the second looked to the future.

It is an amusing piece of irony that the *Cambridge History of American Literature,*[15] designed to show national achievement in scholarship in the national literature, was shaped, as it were, by British precedent. The *Cambridge History of American Literature* was an imitation of the *Cambridge History of English Literature,* which was in turn an imitation of the highly successful political histories issued by that university press. It was edited by a group of Columbia professors, for whose intention one has every respect, but who failed to remember Frederick the Great's description of Joseph II as a monarch who always took the second step before he took the first. The project was consequently haunted by misfortunes. So unorganized was the field, and so careless was the planning of this co-operative enterprise that, part way through publication, it was expanded from three volumes to four—at least, there are four physical books in three volumes, one of which has no bibliographies attached to it. An unfortunate reference in the first edition to Mrs. Eddy as a thrice-married female Hermes Trismegistus offended the Christian Science Church, which forced the publishers to call in the objectionable book and substitute something else. But deeper still lurked the organic weakness of the whole project. There was so little agreement about ends and means that some chapters proved to be nothing more than running book notes, the length of others had small relation to their subject matter, some were devoted to single writers who were no more important than other men crammed into omnibus chapters, and certain units seemed to be the product of amateurs rather than to spring from professional mastery of a specialty. Nevertheless, the *Cambridge History of American Literature* accomplished certain desirable ends. In the first place, it snatched bibliography out of the hands of the book collectors and made it a possession of scholars. In the second place, uneven as the chapters were, they gave an orderly, if wavering, survey of knowledge in the field. In the third place, these volumes were proof that American literary history required a format comparable in dignity to that of the other Cambridge histories. And in the fourth place, the tantalizing inconsistencies in the scheme stimulated scholarship.

The scholars who, at J. B. Hubbell's suggestion, collaborated to produce *A Reinterpretation of American Literature* [16] accepted as a working hypothesis Foerster's theory that, if the great elements creating American literature are European culture and American environment, nevertheless four primary factors shaping its development can be studied—the Puritan tradition, the frontier spirit, romanticism, and realism. Each of these terms was rather a locus of meanings than a completely satisfactory formulation. When, for example, Foerster stated his belief that "the Protestant stamp on American life was primarily Puritan," protests were made by Quaker apologists and others. The frontier appears in the volume largely because of the extraordinary vogue of Turner's essay of 1893 in the United States of the 1920's, but Hubbell, who discussed the topic, frankly admitted that the word was, and is, loosely used. Indeed, when a frontier influence was discovered by some enthusiasts in the international novels of Henry James, a useful hypothesis had been reduced to an absurdity. As for defining romanticism, that was anybody's game, and contributors sought rather to differentiate the American expression of romantic art from its European counterpart than to establish a metaphysic satisfactory to theorists. Finally, realism proved to be a catchall for concepts as different as naturalism, social revolt, muckraking, impressionism, and the psychology of Freud. Yet, vague though the four factors might be, for the first time in the history of the problem a group of competent scholars had agreed, not merely on the elements of their topic, but also on investigating and enriching the terms they had agreed upon; and I think it is not too much to claim that *A Reinterpretation of American Literature* is the key to much that has been written since.

The leading essay in this collection, entitled "A Call for a Literary Historian," had been published by Professor Pattee in 1924,[17] and laid down ten commandments for the new history. Accepting the patent fact that nineteenth-century values would no longer serve, this veteran scholar announced a new era in the academic world; and in three of his ten commandments sketched the salient features of a new history. It was no longer enough, he said, to write an acceptable classroom textbook—American literary history is something that exists in its own right. The success with the general public of Van Wyck Brooks's volumes, beginning with *The Flowering of New England,* shows how shrewdly Pattee gauged the trend of events. Such a book, he also said, must be written against the background of American history—not as a problem in metaphysical theory satisfactory to the Germans, nor with the intention of furthering the moral order, as most of the nineteenth-century studies had done, but as a chronicle of the interrelations between a particular society and its culture. And, he said, the American literary historian must

struggle with the unsettled question as to whether or not literature is really possible in a democracy. The older historians . . . defined it so as to exclude all save *belles* lettres, the aristocratic area of the art. Others, like Wendell, have viewed the field through the atmosphere of the college lecture-room. Higginson, writing on the rise of American literature, began his study with the founding of the *Atlantic Monthly.* The title of the new history should be *A Literary History of the American People.* Such a history has never been written.

The central problem of such a study, he thought, would be to answer these questions:

What has been the effect of attempting to educate the *whole* American mass, to make the reading of books a universal accomplishment? It has raised to a certain degree the general level of the mass, but has it not done so by lowering all the upper levels? [18]

The implication that the peculiar problem of American literary history is the problem of the relation of culture to democracy was further underscored, in the volume, by Arthur M. Schlesinger's essay, designed to show how in the United States the development of literature "is constantly affected by the forces which condition the whole course of social growth. American literary history has as yet received little attention from this point of view." [19]

## 2

In contrast to the assertiveness of Parrington (in *Main Currents*), the tendentiousness of the Marxians, the importunity of Lewisohn, and the mechanical clatter of the *Cambridge History*, the note of the *Reinterpretation* volume was humility. On one point only were the contributors firm; namely, that the old nineteenth-century formulas, apologetic, hortatory, sectional, or pedagogical, would no longer serve an adult nation. Beyond this they would not go. They said, in effect, we do not know the answers to the questions we ask. We need fresh interpretations; we need the "systematic exploitation of promising points of view"; we need to replace the old gentilities by deeper, more detailed studies not hamstrung by obsolete notions of what is aesthetically noble and morally proper; we need to find, in place of the traditional philological structure of graduate work, a frame of reference in which American studies can really fit. Americanists went vigorously to work. In 1929 they created *American Literature*, a quarterly magazine of American literary research, the first one in the country wholly for this purpose. In 1930 they achieved their present degree of autonomy within the Modern Language Association. In 1937 George Washington University in the upper South and Union College in New York state instituted undergraduate programs in the field now commonly known as American civilization. In 1938 Harvard created an advanced program in the graduate school leading to the doctor's degree in this area, and by 1946 some thirty-five institutions had programs, either for undergraduates or for graduates or both, in operation or contemplation. No doubt many of these courses suffer from shallowness, opportunism, and chauvinism; nevertheless, as Europe sinks to the level of a secondary continent and as it is increasingly evident that the United States has become the heir of Europe in that transit of civilization our political historians delight to trace, I believe it to be true that these reforms arise from a deep-seated anxiety to comprehend the responsibility of our culture in the world. And if all this appears to be aside from our main point of the development of a theory of American literary history, we must remember that much of the writing of the last quarter-century has been done in the atmosphere these academic and political revolutions help to create.

A rich variety of studies on American literature and its cultural setting has appeared since the *Reinterpretation* symposium and represents the maturest treatment of the problem we have ever had. Clearly, that problem has not been either to moralize about European literature or to give out first and second prizes to English and American authors, but to comprehend the American environment in which books are written and read. Spatially, the environment is continental; temporally, it is a transition at increasing speeds out of a culture just emerging from medievalism into the industrial culture of the power age; demographically, it is a development from a few Atlantic hamlets homogeneous in religion and race into an imperial population drawn from the four quarters of the globe and comprising every shade of religious belief, racial mixture, and economic status. In this social complex the place of literature changes from one in a Bible-centered community of relatively few readers, to one in an industrial order which invents the two greatest enemies reading as a mass art has yet encountered; namely, the moving picture and the radio. And in the international order this culture proceeds from provincialism to self-confidence and perhaps arrogance. When one ponders the titanic forces at work in American history, one can only admire the innocent hope of previous literary historians that they could settle this sort of problem in preface or opening chapter.

Awareness of complexity has more or less ended the old, shallow, one-volume survey of American literature, Boynton's *Literature and American Life* (1936) [20] being one of the last and best of its kind. Modern scholarship has confined itself to smaller areas in time, space, or subject, and dug deeper, written more carefully, been more aware of historical forces. Some books, of course, are tendentious and popular only, but it is possible to assemble other titles as excellent in critical method, soundness of judgment, and cultural awareness as any work of modern scholarship.

Postulating the self-evident truth that literary criticism in America since T. S. Eliot has altered historical values and that historians are professionally aware of this criticism, we may distinguish three streams in current writing on American literary history. In the first place, the last two or three decades have seen scholarship turning to cultural history; and what was obscurely prophesied in the revolt against gentility has taken shape in books like those of Lewis Mumford, whose *Sticks and Stones* (1924), *Golden Day* (1926), and *Brown Decades* (1931) [21] unite historical learning with aesthetic sensitivity, compel even those who do not agree with him to reconsider their premises, and open vistas on the American scene the nineteenth century never knew. A Baltimore group in *Romanticism in America* (1940) [22] demonstrated how fruitfully the art historian, the philosopher, and the literary historian can work together; and studies by T. C. Hall, Ralph Gabriel, Merle Curti, and Dixon Wecter, not to speak of the *History of American Life* series (1927–1944), [23] are vastly extending our grasp of American cultural development.

In the second place, the study of smaller periods of literary history has been fruitful also. The twenties saw a rash of so-called "decade" books, of which Minnigerode's *Fabulous Forties* (1924) and Beer's *Mauve Decade* (1926) were characteristic. These had the faults of a brash age. But a work like Alfred Kazin's *On Native Grounds* (1942) or F. O. Matthiessen's *American Renaissance* (1941),[24] the one a study of American prose since 1890, the other an examination of leading writers in the time of Emerson and Whitman, is as solid and substantial as a public monument and is not likely soon to be set aside. Moreover, although Tyler is not yet superseded by any notable literary history of the colonial period, studies by Perry Miller, Louis B. Wright, Samuel E. Morison, and others [25] are renewing our sense of the intellectual dignity of the American colonies.

And in the third place, as I have once or twice indicated, the study of the history of ideas and their fortunes in the United States is giving us a better sense of significant values in literature and life. The work of some scholars in this field—Schneider,[26] Riley, Perry, Gabriel, Curti—I have mentioned in other connections. Charvat's *Origins of American Critical Thought* (1936) for the first time put a firm foundation of fact and idea under that hazy subject; studies by Koch and Morais have taught us better to comprehend the deism of the American eighteenth century, and Hofstadter's *Social Darwinism in America* (1944) [27] is a model of scrupulous writing combined with historic range and philosophic grasp. The student of 1950 will have a far more penetrating notion of what American life is and has been than any student has hitherto been able to acquire.

These studies are ancillary to literature, however central they may be to the cultural problem; and it may reasonably be asked, where is the general literary history, comprehensive yet penetrating, for which everyone is looking? The four volumes [28] by Van Wyck Brooks, beginning with *The Flowering of New England* (1936) are, until the new *Literary History of the United States* shall appear, the only general history in the new order we have had. Mr. Brooks has charm and insight and reads widely; he has the unique gift of making the common reader come to like him, and, like Parrington—his opposite in most respects—he has rescued many a name from oblivion. I think it is fair to observe that Mr. Brooks's volumes have been received with more enthusiasm by newspaper reviewers and other tasters of literary wares than they have been by professional scholars; and so many doubts have been cast upon this critic's methodology by specialists that neither his sociology nor his literary appraisals have gone without serious challenge. The battle centers upon Mr. Brooks's intuitive impressionism and upon his haphazard documentation.

From this survey I have excluded, for the sake of clarity, developments in the study of American speech, American folklore, American drama, and American biography, albeit the century has seen good work done in all these fields.

174

Nor have I enumerated the histories of special genres like the short story, the tall tale, the sentimental novel. The admirable labors of Mott and Richardson in the history of American magazines, and one or two excellent works on the history of American criticism I have had to pass over.[29] Presumably the appearance of the *Literary History of the United States* in 1948 will mark the end of an epoch, as the publication of the *Cambridge History of American Literature* thirty years ago marked the end of an earlier era in scholarship. The *Literary History of the United States,* launched as it was only after careful discussion of the nature of the problem, should, one hopes, prove to be a better and richer monument to scholarship than its predecessor.[30]

## 3

In anticipation of its appearance, it is possible to cast a backward glance o'er traveled roads and to reach at least one general conclusion, however tentative. That conclusion is briefly this: *the constant and characteristic element in American literary history has been the search for a formula rather than the solution of a metaphysical problem.*

The second chapter listed a number of hypotheses developed by European scholars about the theory of literary history that have never been applied in the United States. We can, I think, now go further and say that a whole mode of thought on the subject, common enough abroad, has never been domesticated here. This mode of thought I have dubbed metaphysical, and I can quickly illustrate it by turning to the *Britannica* and consulting the article on Benedetto Croce. There one reads,

In its total cognitive function this Spirit manifests itself as art, the first or "dawn" form of knowledge. In this grade it expresses itself in individual embodiments; in so expressing itself it at once creates and beholds what it creates, and has for its objects (which are also its works) whatsoever in experience presents a characteristic individuality.[31]

Whether one accepts or rejects the Crocean theory of art and history, it is patent that no historian of American letters remotely approaches this abstraction. Our scholars have been untouched by the aesthetic of philosophers like Schopenhauer, Hegel, or Santayana. They have made no formal identification of literature and the time spirit, literature and the national soul, literature and the will to live. They have not approached their topic as a problem in the evolution of form, a statement of the absolute, an expression of Faustian knowledge, nor even (at least in these latter days) as the concretion of Christian values.

The formula which tradition has established in the field is probably an inevitable product of the American situation and is tantamount to this question: What has been the relation of literature to society in the United States? The two terms of the equation implied are, as it were, a history of American society and a history of American sensibility; and given the pragmatism apparently characteristic of the American temperament, given the fascination which our complex economic and political development exercises on all observers, it is natural that scholars should have devoted more attention to the sociological relations of literature than to literature as a record of sensibility. In truth, we were launched upon this course from our very beginning. The Puritans were a peculiar people, the record of whose little commonwealths was a record of God's intentions in a redeemed society, and in that society literature was to a high degree part of the recording process. Later on, as we have seen, the theories of Madame de Staël and her contemporaries strengthened a sociological bias. Were not Christianity and republican institutions to produce a glowing literature? Save that our present catchwords have to do with literature and democracy, we have not essentially altered her point of view. Even contemporary criticism, remote from the arena as it prides itself on being, when it adjudges its favorite authors in terms of moral evil and of good, unconsciously accepts, as its ethical problem, the effect of science, warfare, and despair upon modern man in the American state.

When so much emphasis in American scholarship has been thrown upon the sociology of literary history, it may seem surprising if I now remark how naïve much of the interpretation has been. I think I can illustrate what I mean. I remarked in the second chapter that the development of American literature lies wholly in the third of Thienemann's three grand divisions of literary history— the preliteral, the manuscript, and the period of the book. In all times and places somebody has had to support the poet and to pay for copies of what he created if copies were to be made; but in the period of the book, literature has been especially involved in the economic process, until today, without a vast publishing industry, literature as we know it could not exist. It is, moreover, notorious that ideas for books as frequently originate in editorial offices as they do in the brains of authors; and from what we know of seventeenth- and eighteenth-century publishing, remembering men like Tonson, Curll, and Dodsley, we have no reason to suppose that the relation of publisher to author

177

in this regard has essentially altered. The printed book is an object for sale like perfume or theater tickets and is, like them, usually in the luxury class. The complicated relations nowadays of book prices, author's contracts, royalties, publishing discounts, reprint and translation rights to the economic life of the author profoundly affects what he writes and, as the scanty available records of some American publishers indicate, have profoundly affected what he wrote in the past. When we add to these elements the tendency toward gigantism in American publishing, evident in the creation of the book clubs, combinations among publishing enterprises that in an earlier age would have been called trusts, and the existence in the United States of thirty-nine national magazines having a circulation of a million or more, the inference seems irresistible that the economics of publishing has now, and has had in the past, an important influence upon what gets written, printed, and sold.

It would appear that a study of publishing as a business is as basic to the sociology of literature as is the influence of the frontier. Yet this vast area is at the moment almost a barren field, histories of publishing houses being almost invariably books of genteel reminiscence, the publisher-reader-author relationship being well-nigh unexplored territory, and the business fortunes of the book industry having attracted few scholars either in literary history or from schools of business administration. One does not have to be an economic determinist to see the profound importance of this approach to that side of our formula which has to do with the sociology of literary history, since the implications of American publishing business concern everything from imaginative daring in poetry to the express (or implied) control of freedom of thought, utterance, and reading by venture capital, invested funds, family-held securities, and financial tradition. Such things are of the highest consequence.

If we pass to the other side of the formula, to the problem of the history of American sensibility, we find a lesser amount of research being done than in the social approach and also, I fear, a greater degree of bias. Fashions sweep over critics and art historians. A few years ago it was impossible to secure a sympathetic study of the Hudson River school of painting; if today their work is approved, it is now impossible to secure objective, yet sympathetic, judgments on most of the painters who exhibited at the World's Columbian Exposition of 1893. The history of the interpretation of American architecture is a similar tale of violent prejudices held and abandoned. One small informal example will suffice. Ten years ago the old-fashioned American kitchen was utterly condemned, because a kitchen was supposed to be primarily a functioning laboratory; today architects insist that the kitchen be again the center of home living—what it was in Emerson's time.

Fashions also sweep over scholarship and criticism. Critical fashion not only turns to Melville and Henry James and abandons Cooper and Poe, but literary research also tends to project present values backward, throwing, for example, the narrative art of Washington Irving into the shadow of modern disapproval. Scholars by and by grow insensible to the stylistic achievements of men like Hutchinson, Seabury, Otis, and other skilled exponents of public prose in the eighteenth century, because their ears become unconsciously attuned to Crèvecoeur, Woolman, and Tom Paine; they fall into the error of supposing that

179

Poe was vulgar because Aldous Huxley said so, Longfellow juvenile because he was the children's poet, and William Gilmore Simms without art because he did not write like William Faulkner. For all its enormous development in the twentieth century, American criticism has not yet freed itself from the provincialism of time and space, has not yet mastered the truth of Emerson's remark that every scripture should be read in the light of the times that brought it forth, has not yet learned to take pleasure in a catholic variety of literary achievements.

The consequence is that the history of literary sensibility in America—that is, the patient study of what Americans have responded to in art and why they have responded to one expression rather than another—is still to seek. A synthesis like that edited by Professor Boas at Johns Hopkins, *Romanticism in America,* is almost alone in the field, and well-nigh unique in objective sympathy. For the most part, the history of American literature as art is still a battleground of partisan warfare. The South is aggrieved that New York does not share its enthusiasm for southern literature; the West declares that the East is unsympathetic to western talent; the New England scholar has his preoccupations; and so it goes. The continuing difficulty in creating a history of American sensibility is that too many scholars seem more interested in proving what ought to be than in finding out what has been in various epochs of our history. Until we abandon both a patronizing attitude toward forms of art that momentarily seem outmoded, and a partisan attitude toward epochs that seem primary, we shall not progress greatly toward an understanding of American literary development.

It goes without saying that the appearance of the quasi-official *Literary History of the United States* (official in the sense that the resources of the American literature group of the Modern Language Association were at the disposal of the editors) does not mean that scholars shall have rest from their labors. In 1931 Hartley Grattan in the *Bookman* propounded, *à propos* of the *Reinterpretation* volume, a series of problems for "unemployed writers." This was a set of historical queries that needed answering through sound research work; [32] and almost twenty years later some of his problems remain still unsolved, while others have multiplied around them. And as long ago as 1907, in her *Heralds of American Literature,* Annie Russell Marble asked another question which is still in general unanswered: "Why should the writings of this formative era of American federation [1765–1815], the direct impressions and records of the dawning national spirit, be still discounted as American literature?" [33] The fact that Tyler is still the unchallenged "authority" on Revolutionary literature is sufficient comment on this quotation. Indeed, it is still embarrassing to consider how fashion concentrates scholarship on this or that figure, this or that temporal area, to the neglect of great and grave issues. Not to speak of the sorry truth that we have neither established texts nor complete documentation nor competent biographies for an embarrassing number of American figures, how many puzzles still remain unsolved! Why, since we have been so long supposed to have devoted national energy to conquering the country, has literary history been loath to explore the enthralling library of discovery and travel which records this conquest? If one of the glories of French letters is a rich array of memoirs and diarists, why, with a large American library to draw upon—one thinks of John Quincy

Adams, Mayor Hone, Gideon Welles, "Patience Penning-
ton," Jones (the "Rebel War Clerk"), the laconic memoirs
of Grant, the autobiography of Lincoln Steffens—why has
literary history persistently refused to evaluate this kind of
writing after the days of Samuel Sewall? Is there an American way of writing biography, as there is alleged to be a
French way, and if there is, what are its qualities? We know
something about the imaginative energy of Puritanism, but
who has told us fully of the imaginative force in the Quaker
spirit? Or of the Episcopalian tradition in America—of
that church which prides itself upon a cultured ministry,
and which in England has nourished writers as diverse as
Hooker, Vaughan, Bishop Butler, and Dean Inge? Who has
estimated the effect of Roman Catholicism upon the American literary imagination? [34] Who has taken account of the
fruitful Jewish renaissance in this country? Of the vogue
of a utilitarian philosophy among us what do we really
know, once we are past Cotton Mather and Benjamin
Franklin? Or of the effects of Hegelianism upon the American imagination? Or of Schopenhauer, or Royce's idealism,
or the naturalism of Santayana? What of the dynamic concept of nature in American poetry? [35] Is there an American
prose style, and what are its characteristics? Are there continuing concepts of beauty and grace expressed in American writing that historians of ideas do not recognize,
because they are myth and symbol rather than notion and
argument? Why, if the smiling aspects of life are the more
American—and Howells was a shrewd observer—is our
literature so curiously marked by melancholy? Why, in a
gregarious people, this loneliness of the soul? and, among
a kindly one, these sudden imaginative rushes of violence,

brutality, horror, and despair, mirrored in imaginative writing?

4

Problems like these, however fascinating in themselves, belong rather to the tactics than to the strategy of literary history; and the central issue of the study of American literature remains. How shall literary criticism and literary history be fused? If, as this study has revealed, the course of literary history has been stumbling and uncertain, the development of American literary criticism has been equally irregular. As late as 1918, reviewing Bliss Perry's *American Spirit in Literature,* Lawrence Gilman could allege that "our American criticism has not yet wholly outgrown the immaturities that have so long constrained and vitiated it," [36] and H. L. Mencken, who, whatever his prejudices, usually had some support in fact for his indictments, could somewhere remark: "The critical atmosphere in America is an atmosphere of Chopin, raffia work, and the college pump." [37] And if Mr. Mencken be regarded as beyond the pale as expert witness, what shall one reply to Gorham Munson, writing in 1931, who found that the "manipulation of leading ideas in a definite campaign to achieve America's larger cultural objectives" is almost nonexistent in the United States, that the critical revolt of ten or fifteen years earlier had been killed by its own success, and that cultured Americans were compelled to go outside letters for wisdom? [38] The point is not to lament the weakness of the humanist movement, nor to lament with Mencken the "lack of a civilized aristocracy" "delighting in the battle of ideas for its own sake," [39] not to set up T. S. Eliot as a critical pope, nor to create more courses for undergraduates in "criticism," nor to establish more academic quarterlies in which professorial critics may admire or abuse each other. Shocking though it may be to contemporary criticism, our most important duty is still to establish a standpoint in American criticism. It is no good berating the American novel because it is not by Tolstoy or Fielding, or requiring the American poet to write in one narrow "tradition" of technological skill, or scolding American literature because it is not something else, or proclaiming the virtues of Plato and Aristotle—except as you can show them at work in the persons of Lincoln and Webster, Jefferson, Emerson, and Mark Twain. The arbitrary prejudice which finds "values" only in a small list of American authors, especially when these values seldom or never touch upon present problems of culture and the state, deprives the literary historian of the aid of aesthetic insight while concomitantly it impoverishes the general life by keeping "criticism" shut up in the classroom and the quarterly magazine. I think Randolph Bourne was wiser than our own contemporaries when he wrote:

> To come to an intense self-consciousness of the qualities, to feel them in the work of these masters, and to search for them everywhere among the lesser artists and thinkers who are trying to express the soul of this hot chaos of America,—this will be the attainment of culture for us.[40]

We cannot escape responsibility for the conduct of literature in a democracy so sorely beset as our own. It is naïve to misinterpret the struggle of scholars to understand literary history in the American republic as the struggles of inferior minds with inferior material, as if the issue concerned the absolute merits of American writing as against the absolute merits of the literatures of the rest of the world. It is equally naïve to denounce science as an end in itself and then to demand of society that it shall support criticism as an end in itself. Criticism of what? Criticism for whom? Criticism for what cultural and social ends other than a private and mystical self-improvement? And if it be argued that the fascist or the communist state has absorbed the writer and the critic for public ends to the loss of his independence, and that therefore the literary critic in our society has no further responsibility to the commonwealth than to be "critical"—merely to evaluate literary masterpieces according to the light that is in him, and in front of anybody who will listen to him—the retort is crushing and obvious; the truly great critics *have* concerned themselves with public problems and *have* interested themselves in literary history. One has only to glance at the writings of Coleridge, of Arnold, of Sainte-Beuve, of Lessing, of Diderot, to see that this is true. One can understand the revolt against literary scholarship of the historical order, that scholarship in which everything was as important as everything else, but in revolting against Dry-as-Dust our critics have fallen into the company of Zoilus, who is, according to Swift, the descendant of Hybris. But the problem of "Americanism" in literature is no longer the simple cry: "Come out of Europe to be saved"; the problem of the American way of life has become a pressing need for the constant reinterpretation of American cultural values in terms that shall be at once simple enough to be understood and philosophic enough to stand up against pressure from without and reaction from within.

It would be inhuman to expect reform from criticism

and to expect none from the historical scholar. As a class of practicing professional men historical scholars are guilty of most of the offenses charged against them by the critics, and if I do not here rehearse these, it is because the indictment is familiar. They, too, cannot expect support from society merely because scholarship is a good thing in the abstract; since, when scholarship is considered nothing more than a good thing in the abstract, it is inevitably captured by wealth, and its results are lost (except in a remote sense) to the needs of the commonweal. The social setting of literary activity, past and present, is a datum as primary to scholarship as it is to criticism, but the inference to be drawn from this axiomatic truth is not that scholarship must be propagandistic; the proper inference is that scholarship is to have relevance. The historian must of course concern himself with the elements of nationalism in the national letters,[41] but he must learn from the critic how to maintain detachment, sympathetic yet just, from the very element that might otherwise enslave him to the state. He cannot, in the present posture of affairs, agree that any state will do; nor does it follow, in the present posture of affairs, that only the American state and only American literature will do.[42] He will, however, if he be wise, learn from the critic (provided the critic be wise) that the distinction between first-class work and inferior work can never be blurred, if history is to be useful; but he will not, because much American writing is not first-class, therefore infer that the history of American writing is useless to "culture." For if the critic and the historical scholar cannot forget their recent quarrel long enough to tell us how adequate (or inadequate) democratic culture has been in the fostering of literary art, and if they cannot unite on the central problem of evaluating the literary art with which American writers have made their appeal to American men and women, we are in danger either of falling helpless into the mass "media" notion of culture, useful to the police state, or else we shall march farther along the road to Byzantium than most educated Americans care to go.

## NOTES TO CHAPTER VI

[1] The literature of the humanist controversy is vast, repetitious, and abusive. Two significant volumes are *Humanism and America,* ed. Norman Foerster (New York, 1930), and *The Critique of Humanism,* ed. Hartley Grattan (New York, 1930). The famous "debate" in Carnegie Hall in the spring of 1930 among Irving Babbitt, Carl Van Doren, and Henry Seidel Canby seems to have been a failure. See Fred B. Millett, *Contemporary American Authors* (New York, 1940), under the names of the leading humanists, for an extensive survey of controversial articles.

[2] Norman Foerster, "The Literary Historians," *Bookman,* LXXI(4), 365–374 (July, 1930)—and see also his article in the same magazine for September, 1930 (LXXII, 35–44) entitled "The Literary Prophets." Foerster's objection to literary history is twofold: first, it has led scholars to "view literature as a supplement to history"; and, second, it has led the scholar to disparage literary criticism "as, at bottom, subjective and impressionistic." See also his *American Scholar* (Chapel Hill, 1929) a restatement of Irving Babbitt's *Literature and the American College* (New York, 1908), but on another level.

[3] See Clarence Gohdes, "The Study of American Literature in the United States," *English Studies,* XX(2), 61–66 (1938); John T. Flanagan, "American Literature in American Colleges," *College English,* I(6), 513–519 (March, 1940); Guy A. Cardwell, Jr., "On Scholarship and Southern Literature," *South Atlantic Quarterly,* XL(1), 60–72 (January, 1941); Floyd Stovall, "What Price Ameri-

can Literature?" *Sewanee Review*, XLIX(4), 469–475 (October-September, 1941); Bernard De Voto, "The Maturity of American Literature," *Saturday Review of Literature*, XXVII(32), 14–18 (August 5, 1944). Lack of adequate training of prospective teachers of the subject is a common complaint in these articles.

[4] Fred Lewis Pattee, *History of American Literature since 1870* (New York, 1915); Leon Kellner, *American Literature*, translated from the German by Julia Franklin (Garden City, 1915); Woodbridge Riley, *American Philosophy from Puritanism to Pragmatism* (New York, 1915), revised and reissued as *American Thought from Puritanism to Pragmatism and Beyond* (New York, 1923). Kellner's little book, which Mencken found "excellent," has the distinction of opening that critic's epochal essay of 1917, "Puritanism as a Literary Force."

[5] Meredith Nicholson, "The Open Season for American Novelists," *Atlantic*, CXVI(4), 456–466 (October, 1915).

[6] James Bryce, "Stray Thoughts on American Literature," *North American Review*, CCI(712), 357–362 (March, 1915); James Stephens, "The Old Woman's Money," *Century*, XC(1), 48–49 (May, 1915).

[7] These excerpts are, in order, from "Literature and Life," *Century*, XC(2), 318–319 (June, 1915); Florence Finch Kelly, "American Style in American Fiction," *Bookman*, XLI(3), 299–302 (May, 1915); E. W. Garnett, "A Gossip on Criticism," *Atlantic*, CXVII(2), 177 (February, 1916); H. Houston Peckham, "Is Our Literature Still English?" *Sewanee Review*, XXIV(3), 339 (July, 1916); "Secret of American Literature," *Literary Digest*, LVIII(7), 26–27 (August 17, 1918), quoting the New York *Sun;* "America's Literary Future," *Literary Digest*, LXIII(1547), 32 (December 13, 1919), quoting remarks by Clement Shorter and D. Willoughby; St. John Ervine, "Literary Taste in America," *New Republic*, XXIV (305), 144–147 (October 6, 1920); Donald Lawder, "W. L. George on American Literature," *Bookman*, LII(3), 196 (November, 1920); James F. Muirhead, "Must American Literature Defy its Traditions?" *Independent*, CVIII(3809), 270 (March 18, 1922).

[8] Harvey O'Higgins, "Caste in Criticism," *Century*, XCI(5), 662–663 (March, 1916).

[9] "Young English and American Writers," *Literary Digest*, LXIII(7), 30–31 (November 15, 1919), quoting an interview with Gilbert Cannan in the New York *Herald Tribune;* John Middleton

ON NATIVE GROUNDS

Murry, "America and England: A Literary Comparison," *New Republic*, XXIV(301), 41–43 (September 8, 1920).

[10] John Gould Fletcher, "American Poetry," *Literary Review of the New York Evening Post*, IV, 833 (June 21, 1924).

[11] See W. L. George, "Hail Columbia," *Harper's*, CXLII(849), 300–314 (February, 1921); S. K. Ratcliffe, "The Intellectual Reaction in America," *Contemporary Review*, CXXII(679), 14–22 (July, 1922)—this article stems from the famous volume edited by Stearns, *Civilization in the United States*, the kind of book "we do not grow in England"; Virginia Woolf, "American Fiction," *Saturday Review of Literature*, II(1), 1–3 (August 1, 1925).

[12] Cf. George Stuart Gordon, *Anglo-American Literary Relations* (New York and London, 1942), the text of lectures and of fragmentary notes of lectures delivered on the Watson Chair Foundation of the Sulgrave Manor Board, University College, London, in 1931. In 1914 a British committee had discovered that there was no chair of American history, literature, or similar subject in any British university, college, or other institution.

[13] Percy H. Boynton, "Literature in the Light of the War," *English Journal*, VII(2), 77–86 (February, 1918).

[14] Paul Reinsch, "The Inner Freedom of American Intellectual Life," *North American Review*, CCI(714), 733–742 (May, 1915). Whether, as Mr. Reinsch argues, literary scholars in this country have been freer from subconscious postulates than are European scholars, and whether they lack, as he says, a "specific substratum of psychology" are interesting questions.

[15] *Cambridge History of American Literature*, ed. W. P. Trent and others (3 vols. in 4; New York, 1917–1921).

[16] *A Reinterpretation of American Literature: Some Contributions toward the Understanding of Its Historical Development*, ed. Norman Foerster for the American Literature Group of the Modern Language Association (New York, 1928). Besides Foerster, essays were contributed by Fred Lewis Pattee, Jay B. Hubbell, Howard Mumford Jones, Kenneth B. Murdock, Paul Kaufman, Vernon Louis Parrington, Arthur M. Schlesinger, Sr., and Harry Hayden Clark.

[17] In the *American Mercury* (June, 1924).

[18] *Reinterpretation*, pp. 15–16, 17.

[19] *Ibid.*, p. 178.

[20] This volume (Boston, 1936) should not be confused with his earlier *History of American Literature* (Boston, 1919).

189

²¹ All these were published in New York.

²² *Romanticism in America*, ed. George Boas (Baltimore, 1940).

²³ For example, T. C. Hall, *The Religious Background of American Culture* (Boston, 1930); R. H. Gabriel, *The Course of American Democratic Thought* (New York, 1940); Merle Curti, *The Growth of American Thought* (New York, 1943); Dixon Wecter, *The Saga of American Society* (New York, 1937); *History of American Life*, ed. A. M. Schlesinger, Sr., and D. R. Fox (12 vols.; New York, 1927–1944). An additional volume by Dixon Wecter has now appeared.

²⁴ Meade Minnigerode, *The Fabulous Forties* (New York, 1924); Thomas Beer, *The Mauve Decade* (New York, 1926); Alfred Kazin, *On Native Grounds* (New York, 1942); F. O. Matthiessen, *American Renaissance* (New York, 1941).

²⁵ For example, Perry Miller, *The New England Mind: The Seventeenth Century* (New York, 1939); Louis B. Wright, *The First Gentlemen of Virginia* (San Marino, 1940); Samuel E. Morison, *The Puritan Pronaos; Studies in the Intellectual Life of New England in the Seventeenth Century* (New York and London, 1936). Here, as above, I am merely listing representative titles.

²⁶ Herbert W. Schneider, *A History of American Philosophy* (New York, 1946).

²⁷ Gustav A. Koch, *Republican Religion; the American Revolution and the Cult of Reason* (New York, 1933); Herbert Montfort Morais, *Deism in Eighteenth Century America* (New York, 1934); R. Hofstadter, *Social Darwinism in American Thought, 1860–1915* (Philadelphia, 1944).

²⁸ Van Wyck Brooks, *The Flowering of New England, 1815–1865* (New York, 1936); *New England: Indian Summer, 1865–1915* (New York, 1940); *The World of Washington Irving* (New York, 1944); *The Times of Melville and Whitman* (New York, 1947).

²⁹ It may be well to enumerate one or more representative volumes in these fields. In speech, H. L. Mencken, *The American Language*, originally published in 1919 and often revised, is, with its various supplements, too well known to require comment. B. A. Botkin, *A Treasury of American Folklore* (New York, 1944), is representative. A. H. Quinn has written *A History of the American Drama from the Beginning to the Civil War* (New York, 1923), and followed it by a two-volume work bringing the story down to present times (New York, 1927). E. H. O'Neill, *A History of American Biography, 1800–1935* (Philadelphia, 1935), opened a field of investigation that has too few workers in it. F. L. Pattee, *The Development of the Amer-*

*ican Short Story* (New York, 1925), is competent. Herbert Brown, *The Sentimental Novel in America, 1789–1860* (Durham, 1940), explores an aesthetically dreary but historically important field. The development of American magazines can be followed in L. N. Richardson, *A History of Early American Magazines, 1741–1789* (New York, 1931), and F. L. Mott, *A History of American Magazines* (3 vols.; Cambridge, 1938)—the first volume was originally issued by Appleton—a work which descends as far as the eighties of the last century. Morton D. Zabel, *Literary Opinion in America* (New York, 1937), is an anthology of criticism; the introduction is excellent. Of Bernard Smith, *Forces in American Criticism* (New York, 1939), I have spoken briefly in the text. A selected bibliography of leading authorities in the whole field can be found in *Major American Writers*, ed. H. M. Jones and E. E. Leisy (rev. ed.; New York, 1945).

[30] Some of the discussions preceding the actual work on this history are printed in *American Literature*, XII(3), 283–305 (November, 1940)—essays by Louis B. Wright, Harry Hayden Clark, and Yvor Winters; and in R. E. Spiller, "The Task of the Historian of American Literature," *Sewanee Review*, XLIII(1), 70–79 (January–March, 1935).

[31] See, in this connection, the curious article by A. R. Orage, "Unedited Opinions," *New Republic*, XXXIX(505), 299–300 (August 6, 1924) on the relation of Croce to the problem of American literary history.

[32] C. Hartley Grattan, "Wanted: Unemployed Writers," *Bookman*, LXXIII(1), 48–55 (March, 1931).

[33] Annie Russell Marble, *Heralds of American Literature* (Chicago and London, 1907), p. 4.

[34] Such writing on the topic as I have seen seems curiously wooden and usually bogs down in a Catholic inferiority complex or in propaganda. See Katherine Bregy, "American Culture and Catholic Literature," *Catholic World*, CXXVI, 76–84 (Oct., 1927), for a better than average specimen. The author thinks that the way to produce a native group as "distinguished" as Bourget, Bazin, Huysmans, and Jammes is somehow to build up readers in the Catholic church.

[35] The treatment of "nature" by literary historians has been curiously ineffective. See Selden L. Whitcomb, "Nature in Early American Literature," *Sewanee Review*, II(2), 159–179 (February, 1894); Mary E. Woolley, "The Development of the Love of Romantic Scenery in America," *American Historical Review*, III(2), 56–66 (October, 1897); Henry Litchfield West, "American Out-Door

Literature," *Forum*, XXIX(5), 632–640 (July, 1900); J. H. Morse, "American Nature Poetry," *Independent*, LXXII(3316), 1357–1361 (June 20, 1912); Henry Seidel Canby, "Back to Nature," *Yale Review*, VI(4), 755–767 (July, 1917) for specimens. Norman Foerster, *Nature in American Literature* (New York, 1923), is a catalogue of references, plus some consideration of the philosophical rectitude of the poet in question. Amy Lowell thought that nature and man are not separate but one, falling into appropriate place in a vast plan, the key to which is science, and that all modern American poets are affected by this idea, but she does not demonstrate it. See "Pioneering in Poetry," *Independent*, XCVIII(3677), 326 (May 31, 1919).

[36] Lawrence Gilman, "American Literature and Professor Perry," *North American Review*, CCVIII, 915–920 (Dec., 1918).

[37] For a characteristic utterance see H. L. Mencken, "The National Literature," *Yale Review*, IX(4), 804–817 (July, 1920).

[38] Gorham Munson, "American Criticism and the Fighting Hope," *Yale Review*, XX(3), 568–582 (March, 1931).

[39] Mencken, "National Literature," p. 804.

[40] Randolph S. Bourne, "Our Cultural Humility," *Atlantic*, CXIV(4), 507 (October, 1914).

[41] See, on this vexed topic, Harry Hayden Clark, "Nationalism in American Literature," *University of Toronto Quarterly*, II(4), 492–519 (July, 1933); Earl L. Bradsher, "Americanism in Literature," *Sewanee Review*, XXXV(1), 94–102 (January, 1927); Robert Whitney Bolwell, "Concerning the Study of Nationalism in American Literature," *American Literature*, X(4), 405–416 (January, 1939).

[42] In this connection I cite A. C. Ward, *American Literature, 1880–1930* (London, 1932), as a book which seems to me to unite historical scholarship and critical insight.

# The Messenger Lectures

IN ITS ORIGINAL FORM this book consisted of six lectures delivered at Cornell University in December, 1947, namely, the Messenger Lectures on the Evolution of Civilization. That series was founded and its title prescribed by Hiram J. Messenger, B.Litt., Ph.D., of Hartford, Connecticut, who directed in his will that a portion of his estate be given to Cornell University and used to provide annually a "course or courses of lectures on the evolution of civilization, for the special purpose of raising the moral standard of our political, business, and social life." The lectureship was established in 1923.

# Appendix

## SELECTED LIST OF WORKS ON THE HISTORY
## AND PHILOSOPHY OF AMERICAN LITERATURE

1824–25    John Neal. American Writers. [A series of papers contributed to Blackwood's Magazine, repr. and ed. Pattee, Durham, 1937.]

1829    Samuel L. Knapp. Lectures on American Literature. Samuel Kettell. Specimens of American Poetry with Critical and Biographical notices. 3 vols.

1842    Rufus W. Griswold. Poets and Poetry of America.

1846    Rufus W. Griswold. Prose Writers of America.

1848    Rufus W. Griswold. Female Poets of America.

1856    Evert A. and George L. Duyckinck. Cyclopaedia of American Literature. 3 vols.

1878    Moses Coit Tyler. A History of American Literature, 1607–1765. 2 vols.

1885    Edmund C. Stedman. Poets of America.

1886–88    Charles F. Richardson. American Literature, 1607–1885. 2 vols.

1889–90    E. C. Stedman and E. M. Hutchinson. Library of American Literature. 11 vols.

1890    Greenough White. The Philosophy of American Literature.

1894    Henry C. Vedder. American Writers of Today.

1896    F. L. Pattee. A History of American Literature.

1897    Katharine Lee Bates. American Literature.

1897    M. A. DeWolfe Howe. American Bookmen (1898).

Donald Grant Mitchell. American Lands and Letters: The Mayflower to Rip-Van-Winkle.

Moses Coit Tyler. Literary History of the American Revolution. 2 vols.

1898    Henry S. Pancoast. An Introduction to American Literature.

Theodore F. Wolfe. Literary Haunts and Homes.

1899    Mary Fisher. A General Survey of American Literature.

1900    Barrett Wendell. A Literary History of America.

E. C. Stedman. An American Anthology, 1787–1900.

Walter C. Bronson. A Short History of American Literature.

1901    Alphonso G. Newcomer. American Literature.

1902    Lorenzo Sears. American Literature.

1903    Richard Burton. Literary Leaders of America.

T. W. Higginson. Reader's History of American Literature. (With H. W. Boynton.)

William P. Trent. A History of American Literature, 1607–1865.

George E. Woodberry. America in Literature.

1904    Jessie B. Rittenhouse. Younger American Poets.

1906    Leon H. Vincent. American Literary Masters.

1907–23 E. A. Alderman and others, eds., Library of Southern Literature. 16 vols. and a supplementary volume (1923).

1907    L. D. Loshe. The Early American Novel. (Reprinted 1930.)

Annie R. Marble. Heralds of American Literature.

1908    Van Wyck Brooks. The Wine of the Puritans.

Irving Babbitt. Literature and the American College.

1909    William C. Brownell. American Prose Masters.

1912    William B. Cairns. History of American Literature.

W. P. Trent and John Erskine. Great American Writers.

1913    John Macy. The Spirit of American Literature.

1915     F. L. Pattee. History of American Literature Since 1870.

I. Woodbridge Riley. American Thought from Puritanism to Pragmatism and Beyond. (Rev. ed.)

Van Wyck Brooks. America's Coming of Age.

1917–21   Cambridge History of American Literature. 4 vols.

1917     Amy Lowell. Tendencies in Modern American Poetry.

H. L. Mencken. Book of Prefaces.

Stuart P. Sherman. On Contemporary Literature.

1918     Bliss Perry. The American Spirit in Literature.

Van Wyck Brooks. Letters and Leadership.

1919     Louis Untermeyer. The New Era in American Poetry.

James Branch Cabell. Beyond Life.

Waldo Frank. Our America.

Irving Babbitt. Rousseau and Romanticism.

1919–27   H. L. Mencken. Prejudices. 6 vols.

1920     Van Wyck Brooks. The Ordeal of Mark Twain.

H. L. Mencken and George Jean Nathan. The American Credo.

George Santayana. Character and Opinion in the United States.

1921     Carl Van Doren. The American Novel.

1922     Harold E. Stearns (ed.). Civilization in the United States.

Carl Van Doren. The Contemporary American Novel.

1923     Norman Foerster. Nature in American Literature.

D. H. Lawrence. Studies in Classic American Literature.

F. L. Pattee. The Development of the American Short Story.

Stuart P. Sherman. The Genius of America.

Louis Untermeyer. American Poetry since 1900.

Percy H. Boynton. Some Contemporary Americans.

1924     Lewis Mumford. Sticks and Stones.

Irving Babbitt. Democracy and Leadership.

Francis P. Gaines. The Southern Plantation.

1925    Ralph L. Rusk. The Literature of the Middle Western Frontier. 2 vols.

V. F. Calverton. The Newer Spirit.

Van Wyck Brooks. The Pilgrimage of Henry James.

Upton Sinclair. Mammonart.

Jeannette Tandy. Cracker-Box Philosophers.

1926    Stanley Williams. The American Spirit in Letters.

Lewis Mumford. The Golden Day.

Thomas Beer. The Mauve Decade.

Joseph Warren Beach. The Outlook for American Prose.

Dorothy A. Dondore. The Prairie and the Making of America.

1927–30  V. L. Parrington. Main Currents in American Thought. 3 vols.

1927    Lucy L. Hazard. The Frontier in American Literature.

Howard M. Jones. America and French Culture.

Percy H. Boynton. More Contemporary Americans.

Charles and Mary Beard. The Rise of American Civilization. 2 vols. in one.

1928    Norman Foerster and others. A Reinterpretation of American Literature.

Norman Foerster. American Criticism.

Waldo Frank. The Re-discovery of America.

Ernest E. Leisy. American Literature.

Joseph Wood Krutch. The Modern Temper.

Walter Lippmann. Preface to Morals.

Alfred Kreymborg. Our Singing Strength.

1930–38  Frank L. Mott. A History of American Magazines, 1741–1885. 3 vols.

1930    Herbert W. Schneider. The Puritan Mind.

[Twelve Southerners], I'll Take My Stand.

F. L. Pattee. The New American Literature, 1890–1930.

Norman Foerster. Humanism and America.

C. Hartley Grattan. The Critique of Humanism.

Norman Foerster. Towards Standards.

1931      Constance Rourke. American Humor.

Henry S. Canby. Classic Americans.

Lewis Mumford. The Brown Decades.

John Macy. American Writers on American Authors.

George E. DeMille. Literary Criticism in America.

Edmund Wilson. Axel's Castle.

Russell Blankenship. American Literature.

Percy H. Boynton. The Challenge of Modern Criticism.

1932      V. F. Calverton. The Liberation of American Literature.

Ludwig Lewisohn. Expression in America.

Bernard De Voto. Mark Twain's America.

Stuart P. Sherman. The Emotional Discovery of America.

1933      G. A. Koch. Republican Religion.

Granville Hicks. The Great Tradition.

1934      H. M. Morais. Deism in Eighteenth Century America.

H. G. Townsend. Philosophical Ideas in the United States.

Harry Hartwick. The Foreground of American Fiction.

1935      Harlan Hatcher. Creating the Modern American Novel.

F. L. Pattee. The First Century of American Literature.

1936      Samuel E. Morison. The Puritan Pronaos.

Walter Fuller Taylor. History of American Literature.

Van Wyck Brooks. The Flowering of New England.

William Charvat. The Origins of American Critical Thought, 1810–1835.

Arthur Hobson Quinn. History of American Fiction.

Percy H. Boynton. Literature and American Life.

1937      P. Miller and T. H. Johnson. The Puritans.

Morton Zabel. Literary Opinion in America.

Vernon Loggins. I Hear America.

1939    Perry Miller. The New England Mind: The Seventeenth Century.

Bernard Smith. Forces in American Criticism.

1940    Van Wyck Brooks. New England: Indian Summer.

Ralph H. Gabriel. The Course of American Democratic Thought.

G. H. Orians. A Short History of American Literature.

George Boas and others. Romanticism in America.

Carl Van Doren. The American Novel, 1789–1939. (Rev. and enl.)

F. B. Millett. Contemporary American Authors.

1941    Joseph Warren Beach. American Fiction, 1920–1940.

Oscar Cargill. Ideas in America.

F. O. Matthiessen. American Renaissance.

Walter F. Taylor. The Economic Novel in America.

Alfred Kazin. On Native Grounds.

1944    Van Wyck Brooks. The World of Washington Irving.

Richard Hofstadter. Social Darwinism in American Thought.

Howard M. Jones. Ideas in America.

1946    J. L. Blau. American Philosophic Addresses.

Herbert W. Schneider. History of American Philosophy.

Horace Gregory and Marya Zaturenska. History of American Poetry, 1900–1940.

1947    Van Wyck Brooks. The Times of Melville and Whitman.

1948    Robert E. Spiller and others. The Literary History of the United States. 3 vols.

# INDEX

# Index

Adams, Ephraim D., 130
Adams, Henry, 5, 84
Adams, Herbert Baxter, 82, 83
Adams, John Quincy, 49, 50, 181-82
Alison, Archibald, 66
American civilization, programs in, 170-71
American Historical Association, 10, 100, 103, 105
American history, influence of German school on, 82
American literary history:
  Colonial failure, 25 ff., 173
  Early European books on, 68-70
  The "Great Debate," 52 ff., 64, 70-71, 120 ff.
  Idealism in, 98 ff., 128-32
  Latest problems in, 171 ff., 181-87
  Movement of revolt in, 138-50, 183
  Professorships in, 41, 161
  And social history, 176-79
*American Literature* (quarterly), 170
American publishing, history of, 177-79
American school readers, 41, 96, 98-99
American sense of history, 23 ff.
  After Civil War, 80 ff.
American sensibility, problem of, 176, 179-80
*American Whig*, 34-35
Ames, Nathaniel, Jr., 35
Anglo-American literary relations, 36 ff., 58, 66, 79-80, 93-94, 121 ff., 163-65
  *See also* Anglophile tradition; English departments
Anglophile tradition, 49 ff., 80 ff., 97 ff., 131-37, 142, 144
  *See also* Anglo-Saxon racism
Anglo-Saxon, study of, 88 ff.
Anglo-Saxon racism, 20, 83-85, 98-109
Arnold, Matthew, 5, 101, 102, 119, 144, 149, 185
Atherton, Gertrude, 124
*Atlantic Monthly*, 86, 146, 169

Bacon, Francis, 5, 10-14, 53, 59, 60
Balestier, W., 124
Bancroft, George, 55